How to use your Snap Revision Text Guide

This 'Great Expectations' Snap Revision Text Guide will help you get a top mark in your AQA English Literature exam. It is divided into two· easily find help for the bits you find tricky. This book cov to know for the exam:

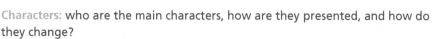

Plot: what happens in the novel?

Setting and Context: what periods, places, events and at understanding the novel?

Characters: who are the main characters, how are they presented, and how do they change?

Themes: what ideas does the author explore in the novel, and how are they shown?

The Exam: what kinds of question will come up in your exam, and how can you get top marks?

To help you get ready for your exam, each two-page topic includes the following key information:

Key Quotations to Learn

Short quotations to memorise that will allow you to analyse in the exam and boost your grade.

Summary

A recap of the most important points covered in the topic.

Sample Analysis

An example of the kind of analysis that the examiner will be looking for.

Quick Test

A quick-fire test to check you can remember the main points from the topic.

Exam Practice

A short writing task so you can practise applying what you've covered in the topic.

Glossary

A handy list of words you will find useful when revising 'Great Expectations' with easy-to-understand definitions.

AUTHOR: CHARLOTTE WOOLLEY

ebook

To access the ebook version of this Snap Revision Text Guide, visit

collins.co.uk/ebooks

and follow the step-by-step instructions.

Published by Collins
An imprint of HarperCollins*Publishers*
1 London Bridge Street,
London, SE1 9GF

HarperCollins*Publishers*
Macken House, 39/40 Mayor Street Upper,
Dublin 1, D01 C9W8, Ireland

© HarperCollins*Publishers* Limited 2018

ISBN 9780008306656

First published 2018
This edition published 2023

10 9 8 7 6 5 4 3 2

British Library Cataloguing in Publication Data.

A CIP record of this book is available from the
British Library.

Printed in the United Kingdom.

Commissioning Editor: Gillian Bowman
Managing Editor: Craig Balfour
Author: Charlotte Woolley
Proofreader: Jill Laidlaw
Project manager and editor:
   Project One Publishing Solutions, Scotland
Typesetting: Jouve
Cover designers: Kneath Associates and
   Sarah Duxbury
Production: Natalia Rebow

ACKNOWLEDGEMENTS

The author and publisher are grateful to the
copyright holders for permission to use quoted
materials and images.

Every effort has been made to trace copyright
holders and obtain their permission for the use of
copyright material. The author and publisher will
gladly receive information enabling them to rectify
any error or omission in subsequent editions. All facts
are correct at time of going to press.

This book is produced from independently certified FSC™ paper
to ensure responsible forest management.

For more information visit: www.harpercollins.co.uk/green

Contents

Part 1: Chapters 1–9

You must be able to: understand what happens in the first chapters of the novel.

How is Pip's family background established?

Pip is brought up 'by hand' by his sister Mrs Joe, who is married to Joe Gargery, the blacksmith. Mrs Joe uses violence to encourage good behaviour but is praised for her patience. Their parents are both dead. Opening the novel with the graveyard establishes a **Gothic** tone, yet Pip narrates with **humour**, describing his impressions of his parents as being 'derived from their tombstones' and the lettering inscribed there.

Pip's relationship with Joe is loving; they are 'ever the best of friends', and commiserate over Mrs Joe's difficult behaviour. When Pip goes to school, he realises Joe has had little education, and tries to teach him what he has learned.

How does Dickens establish Pip's relationship with Magwitch?

In Chapter 1, Pip discovers Magwitch on the marshes. Magwitch uses a made-up story about another convict to frighten Pip into stealing food from the forge. However, Pip discovers a second convict and tells Magwitch he's seen the young man (Compeyson).

Soldiers find the two convicts fighting on the marshes and arrest them. Pip makes it clear to Magwitch that he didn't lead the soldiers there and Magwitch takes responsibility for stealing the food. Weeks later, a third convict meets Pip and Joe in The Three Jolly Bargemen and passes two pounds to Pip, a secret gift from Magwitch.

Dickens uses **caricature** to create memorable details, for example, Magwitch's stifled crying and his use of the iron file make him recognisable later.

What is Pip's relationship with Miss Havisham and Estella?

Miss Havisham asks Pumblechook, Joe's uncle, to bring a boy to Satis House to 'play' with her ward, Estella. Pip is awkward, shy and uncomfortable, and finds Estella very beautiful.

Everything at Satis House has been 'stopped', including Miss Havisham, who wears an old decaying bridal dress. Miss Havisham takes advantage of Pip's discomfort, teasing him and telling Estella that she can 'break his heart'. Estella treats him disdainfully, enjoying making him cry.

Associating with Miss Havisham makes Pip realise the poverty of his upbringing; he wants more. This makes him ashamed, of his background and his dislike of it.

Key Quotations to Learn

[Mrs Joe] concluded by throwing me – I often served as a connubial missile. (Chapter 2)

The man took strong sharp sudden bites, just like the dog. He swallowed, or rather snapped up, every mouthful. (About Magwitch: Chapter 3)

I was too cowardly to do what I knew to be right, as I had been too cowardly to avoid doing what I knew to be wrong. (Chapter 6)

Everything within my view which ought to be white ... had lost its lustre and was faded and yellow. (About Satis House: Chapter 8)

Summary

- Pip, an orphan, meets the convict Magwitch on the marshes, and is persuaded to steal food for him.
- Magwitch finds Compeyson, another escaped convict. They are fighting when they are recaptured by soldiers.
- Miss Havisham invites Pip to 'play' at Satis House with her ward, Estella.
- Pip begins to love Estella and feels ashamed of his upbringing.
- A third convict finds Pip and secretly gives him money.

Questions

QUICK TEST
1. Who is Pip's family?
2. What is Pip's relationship with Magwitch?
3. What is strange about Satis House?
4. What happens at Satis House?
5. Who are the three convicts?

EXAM PRACTICE
Using one or more of the 'Key Quotations to Learn', write a paragraph exploring how Dickens establishes his characters in the first chapters.

Part 1: Chapters 10–19

You must be able to: understand how Dickens develops Pip's character in Chapters 10–19.

How do Pip's relationships develop?

At the beginning of this section, Pip is still a regular visitor to Satis House, including first meeting a 'pale young gentleman' with whom he boxes in the courtyard. He sees the wedding feast, still laid out and rotting on the table, frozen in time.

His family hope that he will be given something in return for his services; when Miss Havisham summons Joe too, she gives him 25 guineas, to apprentice Pip to Joe at the forge, alongside Orlick. Pip feels miserable, out of place, and misses Estella. He feels he is 'restlessly aspiring discontented', unable to find joy in blacksmithing. He also thinks that feeling this way is betraying Joe.

Who is Orlick?

Orlick is another blacksmithing apprentice, who is bitter about Pip's status as Joe's nephew. Orlick feels he is mistreated. He is 'morose', 'ill-favoured' and **misanthropic**. His speech is often violent. He accuses Joe of treating him differently and insults Mrs Joe, calling her a 'foul shrew' and threatening 'I'd hold you under the pump, and choke it out of you.' This leads to a fight between him and Joe, but Joe's strength easily keeps Orlick in check.

How does Pip discover his 'expectations'?

Jaggers finds Pip in the Three Jolly Bargemen and tells him a mysterious benefactor has given him an inheritance. He is to go to London to be educated as a gentleman. The conditions are that his benefactor remain a 'profound secret' and that he always keep the name 'Pip.'

Pip assumes his benefactor is Miss Havisham, preparing him to marry Estella. When he visits to say goodbye – and discovers Estella is gone – Miss Havisham knows all about the benefactor from Jaggers, including the conditions. Her questions lead Pip to believe he is right to think she is his benefactor.

What happens to Mrs Joe?

Mrs Joe is attacked and beaten by an unknown assailant. The assault leaves her severely physically and mentally disabled. Afterwards, she keeps drawing a hammer symbol (she can't speak) and appears like a 'child towards a hard master' when Orlick visits her.

Key Quotations to Learn

The black beetles … groped about the hearth in a ponderous elderly way. (Chapter 11)

He pulled up his shirt-collar so very high behind, that it made the hair on the crown of his head stand up like a tuft of feathers. (About Joe: Chapter 13)

I wanted to make Joe less ignorant and common, that he might be worthier of my society and less open to Estella's reproach. (Chapter 15)

It was an uneasy bed now, and I never slept the old sound sleep in it any more. (Chapter 18)

My dream was out; my wild fancy was surpassed by sober reality; Miss Havisham was going to make my fortune on a grand scale. (Chapter 18)

Summary

- Pip feels restless in his old life, seeing it through Estella's eyes.
- He feels guilty about this.
- Jaggers tells him he has 'expectations': a mysterious inheritance.
- Pip believes Miss Havisham is his benefactor.
- Mrs Joe is attacked and left for dead.

Questions

QUICK TEST
1. How does Pip feel about becoming an apprentice?
2. What are the conditions of Pip's 'expectations' (his inheritance)?
3. Who is Orlick?
4. What happens to Mrs Joe?

EXAM PRACTICE
Using one or more of the 'Key Quotations to Learn', write a paragraph exploring how Pip's attitudes to life change after meeting Estella.

Part 2: Chapters 20–29

You must be able to: understand how Dickens develops his themes and ideas in Chapters 20–29.

What happens to Pip in London?

Pip begins to make friends and receive a different education. Jaggers gives him a substantial allowance, although he knows Pip will 'go wrong' and must find his own way. Wemmick, Jaggers' assistant, takes Pip to Herbert Pocket's rooms where Pip is surprised to recognise his new roommate – Herbert is the 'pale young gentleman' he fought at Satis House. Herbert tells him Miss Havisham's story, including that she brought Estella up to 'wreak revenge on all the male sex'.

Mr Pocket (Herbert's father) tutors Pip alongside Herbert and other young men including Startop and Bentley Drummle. The loving chaos of the Pocket household – 'tumbling up' amidst laughter – sharply **contrasts** the Havishams' coldness, highlighting their dysfunction.

How does Pip's relationship with Estella develop?

Pip returns to see Estella and is still completely in love with her. She has become a beautiful young woman, but is cold, haughty, with an air of 'completeness and superiority' that make him realise his 'youthfulness and submission' in contrast. She reminds him of someone, but he doesn't realise that it is Molly, Jaggers' housekeeper, whose hands Jaggers draws attention to when they have dinner.

How does Pip's relationship with Joe change?

Joe visits Pip in London dressed in his holiday best. He plays awkwardly with his hat and muddles his speech. Dickens uses non-standard grammar – 'drawed' and 'growed' – and Joe's dialect ('Miss A' for Miss Havisham) to show his lack of education. Pip sees him as clumsy and **uncouth**. Joe is uncomfortable in London, and in Herbert's presence. Pip is embarrassed by Joe's behaviour, which demonstrates his lesser education and the differences that now exist between them.

Joe recognises Pip's discomfort. He tells Pip he should remember Joe at the forge, and not feel guilty he doesn't want Joe in his new London life. When Pip visits Estella, he does not stay at the forge.

Pip's sense of superiority extends to others; he finds Orlick working at Satis House, but asks Jaggers to fire him because he is 'not the right sort' to be associated with the household.

Key Quotations to Learn

'I'm wrong in these clothes. I'm wrong out of the forge, the kitchen, or off th' meshes.' (Joe: Chapter 27)

Truly it was impossible to dissociate her presence from all those wretched hankerings after money and gentility that had disturbed my boyhood. (Pip on Estella: Chapter 28)

All other swindlers upon earth are nothing to the self-swindlers. (Chapter 28)

Summary

- In London, Pip meets Jaggers, Wemmick, and Herbert Pocket.
- Pip sees Estella again and is still in love with her.
- Joe visits Pip in London but is awkward and doesn't fit Pip's new expectations.
- Pip feels ashamed of Joe and stays elsewhere when he visits Satis House.

Sample Analysis

Dickens uses **macabre** settings to convey Pip's discomfort in London and to **foreshadow** the difficult experiences he will have. On his first day Pip visits Smithfield, a meat market which is 'asmear with filth and fat and blood and foam [which] seemed to stick to [Pip]'. The grim **syndetic** list creates a gruesome impression of death. The verb 'stick' implies that it is inescapable, that people cannot avoid reality no matter how harsh.

Questions

QUICK TEST
1. Who does Pip meet when first in London?
2. What does the difference between the Pockets and the Havishams show?
3. What changes between Pip and Joe?
4. What is Estella like now?

EXAM PRACTICE
Using one or more of the 'Key Quotations to Learn', write a paragraph exploring how Dickens presents ideas about the changes in Pip's life, relationships or attitudes since being in London.

You must be able to: understand how Dickens develops Pip's relationships in Chapters 30–39.

How do Pip's relationships with Herbert and Wemmick progress?

They become closer friends. Pip has an inflated sense of his ability; he thinks he is 'prompt, decisive, energetic, clear, cool-headed', making him a bad influence on Herbert, running up excessive debt. However, Pip secretly buys Herbert a job to help his friend's ambitions.

Wemmick has a mock-castle home he constructed himself. He insists on a clear separation between home and work.

How does Pip's character change?

Approximately five years pass in this section. Pip comes of age but is unhappy: he spends too much and doesn't work. He regularly visits Satis House but is miserable when Estella meets Bentley Drummle. He witnesses Estella's rejection of Miss Havisham, saying she cannot love her: 'my gratitude and duty cannot do impossibilities'.

Pip returns for Mrs Joe's funeral. Mourners are **obsequious** towards Pip, but Joe is side-lined in a corner. The funeral is more extravagant than Joe wanted, with coffin-bearers wearing elaborate mourning clothes 'like a blind monster with twelve legs', because Mr Pumblechook believed it more suitable.

Biddy has been living at the forge to care for Mrs Joe. She and Joe are awkward with Pip, treating him as a guest rather than as family. Pip is condescending when Biddy implies he has mistreated Joe. By the end of the section, Pip expects he won't return to the forge.

What is the truth about Pip's expectations?

In Chapter 39, Magwitch arrives secretly. Pip is horrified to be associated with criminality but Magwitch reveals he is Pip's benefactor. Pip is shocked and panicked: 'I seemed to be suffocating.'

He is devastated to think 'how wrecked I was, and how the ship in which I had sailed was gone to pieces' as all his hopes regarding Estella were built on false foundations. He is ashamed of his treatment of others, realising his wealth doesn't make him special.

Key Quotations to Learn

There was a gay fiction among us that we were constantly enjoying ourselves, and a skeleton truth that we never did. (Chapter 34)

Biddy, Joe, and I ... dined in the best parlour, not in the old kitchen. (Chapter 35)

[As] though she were devouring the beautiful creature she had reared. (Pip, on Miss Havisham: Chapter 38)

'If I gets liberty and money, I'll make that boy a gentleman!' (Magwitch: Chapter 39)

Summary

- Pip is a bad influence on Herbert; they get into debt.
- Pip grows closer to Wemmick.
- Pip is unhappy, missing Estella and unable to settle in his new life.
- Mrs Joe dies. At the funeral Pip is treated as a guest rather than as family.
- Magwitch arrives back in London and reveals he is Pip's benefactor.

Sample Analysis

Pip's efforts to leave his old life behind are **symbolised** in the money he exchanges with Magwitch. Pip repays Magwitch with two 'clean and new' notes, symbolising the purity he feels his wealth has. Earlier, he receives notes from Magwitch that are 'crumpled', 'sweltering' with the 'warmest intimacy [of] cattle-markets', symbolic of the criminality that Pip feels dirties them, and him by association. Magwitch, however, burns the notes, a grand gesture indicating his wealth but also perhaps foreshadowing how easy it will be for them to lose everything.

Questions

QUICK TEST
1. How does Pip's relationship with Herbert develop?
2. What happens to Mrs Joe?
3. What is the truth of Pip's expectations?
4. How has Pip changed during this section?

EXAM PRACTICE
Using one or more of the 'Key Quotations to Learn', write a paragraph exploring the way Dickens develops his themes during these chapters.

Part 3: Chapters 40–49

You must be able to: understand how Dickens develops relationships and themes in Chapters 40–49.

How does Dickens create sympathy for Magwitch?

Magwitch's story suggests he was abandoned by society, his life inevitably leading to crime. He was rejected as a child and uneducated. Having been in prison, he was treated as a life-long criminal, a lesser human being.

He worked with Compeyson on forgeries. Compeyson then used their class differences in court to ensure Magwitch took the blame. Herbert realises that Compeyson is 'Arthur', who defrauded Miss Havisham. When Magwitch escaped the Hulks, he was sentenced to **transportation**.

In Australia he became a wealthy sheep breeder, which implies he could have been successful in Britain with the right start in life. He considered Pip a son, deciding to make him a gentleman. This ambition motivated Magwitch to improve himself further.

Pip is miserable and frightened with Magwitch in his home: 'I doubt if a ghost could have been more terrible to me', despite Magwitch's efforts to help him and his evident love for Pip.

Pip decides that he can no longer take any of Magwitch's money. Although at first horrified by Magwitch and his origins, he becomes fond of him.

What does Pip discover about Estella?

Estella marries Bentley Drummle; she reminds Pip it is not in her nature to love and that she warned him she would never return his feelings.

Pip realises that Molly is Estella's mother, recognising Molly's hands and eyes as Estella's could be 'after twenty years of a brutal husband and a stormy life'.

What happens to Miss Havisham?

Pip confronts her about leading him to believe she was his benefactor, and her cruelty towards Estella. She admits it, though says he would have 'compassion and understanding' if he knew her story. She asks for his forgiveness, repeating 'What have I done!'

He forgives her but says she should repair the damage done to Estella. He feels sympathy for her, understanding the damage she has also done to herself.

As Pip leaves, he imagines Miss Havisham hanging from a beam and is so disturbed he returns to see she is safe. As he watches, Miss Havisham's dress sets on fire. Pip puts the fire out, but she is badly injured. She is 'insensible' when he visits her, muttering for his forgiveness.

Key Quotations to Learn

The more I dressed him and the better I dressed him, the more he looked like the slouching fugitive on the marshes. (On Magwitch: Chapter 40)

'Who am I, for God's sake, that I should be kind?' (Miss Havisham: Chapter 44)

'I am tired of the life I have led, which has very few charms for me, and I am willing enough to change it.' (Estella: Chapter 44)

She had secluded herself from a thousand natural and healing influences; that, her mind, brooding solitary, had grown diseased. (On Miss Havisham: Chapter 49)

Summary

- Magwitch has made a fortune as a sheep farmer, motivated by thoughts of making Pip a gentleman.
- Herbert realises that Compeyson is the man who pretended to love Miss Havisham.
- Pip decides to take no more money from Magwitch.
- Pip realises that Molly is Estella's mother.
- Miss Havisham asks Pip's forgiveness.
- Miss Havisham's dress is set alight, which fatally injures her.

Questions

QUICK TEST
1. What is the connection between Compeyson, Miss Havisham and Magwitch?
2. How does Pip realise Molly is Estella's mother?
3. What happens to Estella?
4. What happens between Pip and Miss Havisham?
5. What happens to Miss Havisham?

EXAM PRACTICE
Using one or more of the 'Key Quotations to Learn', write a paragraph explaining how Dickens presents ideas about how people's environments shape their behaviour.

Part 3: Chapters 50–59

You must be able to: understand how Dickens creates a sense of **resolution** in Chapters 50–59.

What happens to Magwitch?

Pip, Herbert and Startop try to smuggle Magwitch to London then out of the country. Magwitch is resigned but happy that Pip will continue a gentleman ('I've seen my boy, and he can be a gentleman without me'). Compeyson leads the customs officers to them. They fight – Compeyson is drowned and Magwitch is seriously injured.

Pip realises that Magwitch is Molly's common-law husband, and therefore Estella's father. As Magwitch is dying in prison, Pip tells him that he has found his daughter: 'She is a lady and very beautiful. And I love her!' Magwitch never knows that Pip can't inherit his fortune when he dies. His final moments are peaceful and contented, kissing Pip's hand and dying holding it.

How does Pip's relationship with Biddy and Joe heal?

Pip falls ill and is nearly arrested for his debts. Someone informs Joe, who comes to London to care for him. As Pip begins to recover Joe becomes more distant, calling him 'sir' again. When recovered, Pip wakes one morning to find that Joe has gone but left a note saying all his debts have been paid.

Pip decides that, now he is penniless, he will propose to Biddy and offer to live wherever she wishes. However, when he gets to the forge he realises it is Biddy and Joe's wedding day.

What happens between Pip and Orlick?

Pip receives a letter instructing him to go to the marshes. It is an ambush by Orlick. Orlick traps him and confesses to killing Mrs Joe: 'I giv' it her! I left her for dead.' He tries to kill Pip, before Herbert arrives with Trabb's boy to rescue him. Orlick has been jealous of Pip since childhood, claiming he could have 'chucked you away dead' and blames him for losing his job at Satis, and his lack of success with Biddy. He has worked with Compeyson, following Magwitch and planning to destroy them both.

What happens at the end?

Eleven years pass. Herbert and Pip are businessmen, working hard and making a profit. Joe and Biddy are happily married with a child named Pip.

Pip has heard that Estella's marriage was unhappy, possibly violent. Drummle died in an accident several years before. Pip goes to the ruins of Satis House and finds Estella there. They agree to be friends and leave together.

Key Quotations to Learn

'We can no more see to the bottom of the next few hours than we can see to the bottom of this river what I catches hold of.' (Magwitch: Chapter 54)

The June weather was delicious. The sky was blue, the larks were soaring high over the green corn, I thought all that countryside more beautiful and peaceful by far than I had ever known. (Chapter 58)

I saw no shadow of another parting from her. (Chapter 59)

Summary

- Pip, Herbert and Startop try to smuggle Magwitch out of England.
- Compeyson identifies them. In a fight, he is drowned, and Magwitch is fatally injured.
- Pip tells Magwitch that his daughter (Estella) is alive and that he loves her.
- Orlick attempts to kill Pip.
- Pip returns to Satis House and reconciles with Estella.

Questions

QUICK TEST
1. What happens during Magwitch's escape?
2. How does Pip's relationship with Joe progress?
3. What does Orlick do?
4. What happens between Pip and Estella at the end?

EXAM PRACTICE
Using one or more of the 'Key Quotations to Learn', write a paragraph explaining how Dickens creates a sense of resolution in the last section.

Narrative Structure

You must be able to: explain how Dickens structures his story.

What is the overall structure?

Dickens wrote three distinct sections: Pip's childhood; Pip's expectations and his youth in London; Pip's maturity after Magwitch returns and reveals the truth.

What is a *bildungsroman*?

A *bildungsroman* is a story about the experience of moving from childhood to adulthood. It is often, as in *Great Expectations*, written in the first person by the **protagonist** as an adult, looking back on their childhood and experiences growing up.

How does Dickens use cliffhangers?

Great Expectations was **serialised** in weekly instalments. Every two or three chapters there is a **cliffhanger** to maintain the readers' excitement for the next week.

For example, the first instalment ends at Chapter 2, when Pip is taking Magwitch the stolen food. This leaves readers waiting for the next instalment to see what will happen when he gets there, and what the convict might do to him.

How does Dickens create Pip's narrative voice?

Dickens uses a **dual narrative**, giving the adult-Pip and the child-Pip their own **narrative voices**. The story is narrated by adult-Pip looking back. Dickens uses authorial **interjections** where adult-Pip comments on thoughts, feelings and behaviours of child-Pip. These are critical, comic, **reflective** or **sarcastic**. They might create **pathos** for child-Pip. When child-Pip is feeling ashamed of home, adult-Pip concludes that: 'The change was made in me; the thing was done. Well or ill done, excusably or inexcusably, it was done.' This recognition is only possible after the event but guides the reader's interpretation of the changes in child-Pip's character.

For example, when Pip begins to feel ashamed of home, adult-Pip comments: 'Pause you who read this, and think for a moment of the long chain of iron or gold, of thorns and flowers, that would never have bound you, but for the formation of the first link on one memorable day.' The direct address and the reference to a 'chain' suggests he views this moment as starting him on a path only visible when looking back. The reflective tone encourages us instead to have sympathy, because child-Pip was unaware of the consequences.

Key Quotations to Learn

I have often thought that few people know what secrecy there is in the young under terror. (Chapter 2)

It is the same with any life. Imagine one selected day struck out of it, and think how different its course would have been. (Chapter 9)

Whatever I acquired, I tried to impart to Joe. This statement sounds so well, that I cannot in my conscience let it pass unexplained. (Chapter 14)

I must give one chapter to Estella. It is not much to give to the theme that so long filled my heart. (Chapter 37)

Summary

- Dickens wrote three sections: childhood, expectations, and maturity.
- A *bildungsroman* is a story about growing up.
- Cliffhangers are used to maintain interest between instalments.
- Adult-Pip sometimes comments on his younger actions to create humour or sympathy.

Sample Analysis

Dickens' dual narrative creates sympathy for child-Pip. In Chapter 1, adult-Pip writes: 'the small bundle of shivers growing afraid of it all and beginning to cry, was Pip.' The adjectives 'small' and 'afraid' make the child seem very young, and create pathos, yet 'bundle of shivers' introduces a comic tone suggesting this is his defining feature, as though adult-Pip is looking back fondly at his old self.

Questions

QUICK TEST
1. What three sections does Dickens write?
2. What is a *bildungsroman*?
3. What is a reason for cliffhangers?
4. What is the effect of the adult narrator looking back?

EXAM PRACTICE
Using at least one of the 'Key Quotations to Learn', write a paragraph explaining the impact of Dickens' narrative structure.

Setting and Timing

You must be able to: understand the setting and timings of the novel.

When is the novel written and set?

Dickens published *Great Expectations* in 1861, the time when Pip is writing. It is set in the early 1800s, a time in which Britain changed dramatically during the Industrial Revolution. Cities like London expanded rapidly.

Dickens writes **nostalgically** about the rural setting of Joe's forge. By the 1860s, many such villages felt under threat by newly industrialised cities. Places like the forge were at risk from factory production and mechanisation.

Dickens also uses the backdrop of an expanding British Empire, for example, in Herbert and Pip's jobs in Cairo, Egypt, as shipping clerks, and the busy shipping routes on which they try to smuggle Magwitch.

What is the significance of the marshes?

Dickens uses **pathetic fallacy** to echo Pip's emotions. His home is not idyllic and rural, but difficult and unpleasant. When he is frightened, mists descend on the marshes and cloud his judgement. The marshes are somewhere secrets can hide and the Hulks loom threateningly over the landscape. By the end of the novel there is a June-blue sky above.

What is the significance of London?

Dickens contrasts Pip's rural upbringing with London. The Industrial Revolution had caused overcrowding, with industrial and residential buildings together. There was poor sanitation and air quality, and dilapidation caused by too many people living together in small spaces.

Pip finds London dirty and disgusting. Dickens is commenting on social standards. Not even Pip's money is enough for him to have a pleasant home in London. The filthiness of London foreshadows the moral difficulties Pip experiences there.

Dickens gives extremely specific references, for example, juxtaposing the Smithfield meat market with Newgate Prison on Pip's arrival, linking the commercialism of the city with the deaths of criminals.

What does Satis House symbolise?

Satis House is decaying and lost in time. It has 'a great many iron bars', is 'empty and disused'. It has **connotations** of a **tragic** fairy tale with Gothic **imagery** as it is 'hidden in cobwebs' and infested by mice. This decay echoes the living ghosts (Estella and Miss Havisham) inhabiting it. Pip notices the 'cold wind seemed to blow colder there than outside the gate.'

By the end there is 'no house now … no building whatever left.' With Miss Havisham's death, Satis House has disappeared entirely.

Key Quotations to Learn

The marshes were just a long black horizontal line … the sky was just a row of long angry red lines and dense black lines intermixed. (Chapter 1)

Some of the windows had been walled up; of those that remained, all the lower were rustily barred. (About Satis House: Chapter 8)

We were disgorged by an introductory passage into a melancholy little square that looked to me like a flat burying-ground. (About Barnard's Inn: Chapter 21)

It was wretched weather; stormy and wet, stormy and wet; and mud, mud, mud, deep in all the streets. (Chapter 39)

Summary

- The novel is written in 1861, with Pip reflecting on his childhood.
- Pathetic fallacy echoes Pip's emotions.
- London's dirt and discomfort foreshadows Pip's difficulties there.
- Satis House is **reminiscent** of a Gothic fairy tale; its ruin is a physical **representation** of Miss Havisham's decline.

Sample Analysis

Dickens presents London as busy, dirty and unpleasant. Pip describes it as 'ugly, crooked, narrow and dirty' (Chapter 20), the list of adjectives portraying it as somewhere that contrasts sharply with his rural upbringing, and the impression of the city as somewhere to make a fortune. Even with Pip's inheritance, he finds his rooms dingy, small and crowded, suggesting that a fortune is needed to live a good comfortable life there.

Questions

QUICK TEST
1. When is the novel written and set?
2. How does Dickens use pathetic fallacy in his representation of the marshes?
3. What does London symbolise?
4. What does Satis House represent?

EXAM PRACTICE
Relating your ideas to at least one of the 'Key Quotations to Learn', explore the way that Dickens uses the settings of the novel.

Dickens' Background and Literary Style

You must be able to: explain the significance of different literary styles and influences.

How like Dickens is Pip?

Dickens uses some **autobiographical** details in writing Pip's early life – Dickens, like Pip, worked in a job he hated. Because his father was in debtor's prison when Dickens was 12, Dickens had to work in a boot-blacking factory to pay off the debt. Like Pip, he thought he could do better. Dickens also went to London at a young age (nine) and made a success of himself through education, becoming a law clerk, then reporter, then novelist and publisher.

This perhaps explains Dickens' tone sometimes when the narrator looks back at the young Pip with fondness, but also critically; in a way, Dickens is looking back at his younger self, too.

What is social realism?

Social realism is when novelists draw on real-life experiences or situations in order to create **empathy** for issues, such as poverty, its relationship to crime, and the life of the working class. For Dickens, his writing was a crucial way to spread awareness of the dire situations many poor people found themselves in and to make an argument for ending poverty and to improve the treatment of orphans. He found he could make his ideas more memorable and convincing for some by using fiction.

Great Expectations does this through its sympathetic description of criminals such as Magwitch, and the exploration of the provision for orphans. Pip is constantly aware that his 'expectations' are the only way to change his future; even when Joe suggests getting an education it's only really so he can become a better blacksmith.

Key Quotations to Learn

'But what the Devil was I to do? I must put something into my stomach, mustn't I?' (Magwitch, Chapter 42)

'I noticed first of all what a gentleman Compeyson looked, wi' his curly hair and his black clothes and his white pocket-handkercher, and what a common sort of a wretch I looked.' (Magwitch, Chapter 42)

Summary

- Pip and Dickens had difficult childhood experiences and felt out of place.
- Like Pip, Dickens went to London at a young age.
- Social realism uses real-life experiences to highlight the inequalities in society.
- Dickens uses *Great Expectations* to criticise Victorian attitudes towards criminals and orphans.

Sample Analysis

Dickens' social realism includes his criticism of the legal system for trying children in the same way as adults. Jaggers angrily says, 'Put the case that he often saw children solemnly tried at a criminal bar, where they were held up to be seen'. The adverb 'solemnly' conveys a sense of anger, that the legal system takes this seriously, seeing them as criminals rather than children in need of help to improve their lives. That they are 'held up' could be taken literally, as it emphasises their smallness (partly due to malnourishment and poverty, as well as their age), making them seem more vulnerable. Being 'held up' also has connotations of being deliberately put on display, so the legal system is seen to be doing what it considers the 'right thing'.

Questions

QUICK TEST
1. What was Dickens' childhood like?
2. What elements of Dickens' childhood are reflected in his portrayal of Pip?
3. What is social realism?
4. What issues is Dickens exploring through the novel?

EXAM PRACTICE
Write a paragraph explaining how Dickens' writing is influenced by his background or his use of social realism.

Victorian Orphans and Criminals

You must be able to: understand how Dickens' writing is influenced by contemporary attitudes.

What were Victorian attitudes towards orphans?

Many people assumed orphans were a drain on society, as they needed looking after, housing and feeding. They were also perceived as more likely to become criminals because of their unstable lives. Many wanted social reform to stop this happening, including setting up workhouses or boarding schools to house orphans. These were often cruel, harsh places, aimed at 'correcting' the children, treating them as though they were already criminals.

What was Dickens' attitude towards orphans?

Dickens wanted to explore social attitudes to orphans and to influence their treatment. He drew attention to children's need for moral examples and kind influences. By contrasting Miss Havisham's adoption of Estella, which is **characterised** by mental and emotional cruelty, with Joe's mentoring of Pip, which displays kindness and care, he showed that a good adoptive parent and role model can help a child become a good adult.

What were Victorian attitudes towards criminals?

Crime was problematic in cities where poverty and overcrowding were common. Victorians could be **callous**, thinking that criminals were born, not made through their circumstances. Dickens uses Magwitch to contradict this idea.

Magwitch is first locked up in the Hulks, large ships moored 'like a wicked Noah's ark', which temporarily housed prisoners. Magwitch is then transported to Australia (for life), like approximately 160,000 other convicts.

Crime fascinated the Victorians and was sometimes **lurid** entertainment. Mr Wopsle re-enacts crime reports, 'gloating over every abhorrent adjective'. Tourists viewed the Hulks and Newgate Prison, as Pip does. Victorian literature also introduced detective and mystery **genres**. Dickens describes Magwitch's trial as taking place in front of a 'large theatrical audience'.

How does Dickens connect orphans and criminals in the novel?

Magwitch was an orphan, and he describes himself as a 'ragged little creetur', who 'got the name of being hardened' in a cycle that keeps him trapped in prison and crime. Part of his motivation for making Pip a gentleman is to revenge himself against the system that kept him trapped, but it is also to rescue Pip from a possible similar fate.

Although Estella is not an orphan – her parents Molly and Magwitch are still alive – her adoption by Miss Havisham places her in a similar position to Pip after Magwitch's intervention. Jaggers argues that he did this partly to save her, and to save Molly when defending her against her murder charge. Estella is presented as a character who could be 'saved' from the 'heap' that Magwitch was in, yet she has suffered in other ways.

Key Quotations to Learn

[Pip was] brought up by hand. (Chapter 1)

'Others on 'em giv me tracts what I couldn't read, and made me speeches what I couldn't understand.' (Magwitch, on his upbringing: Chapter 42)

'Tramping, begging, thieving, working sometimes when I could, – though that warn't as often as you may think, till you put the question whether you would ha' been over-ready to give me work yourselves.' (Magwitch: Chapter 42)

'All the children he saw … he had reason to look upon as so much spawn, to develop into the fish that were to come to his net.' (Jaggers: Chapter 51)

'Here was one pretty little child out of the heap who could be saved.' (Jaggers, on Estella: Chapter 51)

Summary

- Victorians saw orphans as a drain on society.
- Poverty and overcrowding led to crime.
- Criminals were harshly punished, including by life-long transportation to Australia.
- Many Victorians thought criminals were born, not made through circumstance.

Sample Analysis

Dickens makes the Hulks sound threatening: 'moored by massive rusty chains, the prison-ship seemed in my young eyes to be ironed like the prisoners.' The adjective 'barred' and **simile** 'ironed like the prisoners' suggest the Hulks are a **personification** of the prisoners themselves. The chains represent the terrible conditions inside. The 'rusty' nature of the chains implies they have been there a long time. Like the ship, the prisoners have no hope of escape as society won't accept them.

Questions

QUICK TEST
1. What were Victorian attitudes to orphans?
2. Why does Dickens write about orphans?
3. What were Victorian attitudes to criminals?
4. How does Dickens connect orphans and criminals?

EXAM PRACTICE
Relating your ideas to at least one of the 'Key Quotations to Learn', explore the way that Dickens presents either criminals or orphans in the novel.

You must be able to: analyse the way that Dickens presents Pip.

How does Dickens present Pip's innocence?

Pip is 'dreadfully frightened' when he meets Magwitch. He later asks his sister 'what's Hulks?', showing his life is sheltered from crime. Stealing from Mrs Joe reveals, rather than destroys, his innocence. He is anxious and tormented by guilt.

How does Pip's innocence disappear?

Estella's insults 'coarse' and 'common' draw attention to their differences. She gives him food on the floor like a 'dog in disgrace' and he sees himself as 'vulgar' for the first time. He begins to aspire to a life she would approve of.

How is Pip changed by his inheritance?

Money brings him unhappiness. He is always 'more or less miserable' and Estella is 'inseparable from all my restlessness'. He doesn't fit into his new society, spends too much money and becomes arrogant. He becomes an unlikable character, redeemed only through loving Estella, and adult-Pip's interjections describing his unhappiness.

How does Dickens use Magwitch's return as a turning point for Pip?

Pip is 'resentful' and 'reluctant' when Magwitch returns. He tries to give him money to leave despite his near-starvation. The adult Pip feels a 'touch of reproach' when he speaks harshly, and apologises.

The truth is a turning point. It destroys Pip's dreams and forces him to face reality. It also makes him realise his 'worthless conduct' towards Joe, and that he could 'never, never undo what [he] had done.'

How does Pip grow up?

He becomes determined to become a moral man. Taking no more of Magwitch's money symbolises his desire for a moral life free from any 'taint' of crime. He also learns to treat people fairly and respectfully. He tells Miss Havisham she is not responsible for his misery: 'I want forgiveness and direction too much to be bitter with you.' He is similarly generous to Magwitch: 'I will be as true to you as you have been to me!'

Pip has come to realise that money is unimportant; morality and kindness are important above all as the marks of a true gentleman.

Key Quotations to Learn

[Bundle] of shivers ... (Pip, describing himself: Chapter 1)

Her contempt for me was so strong, that it became infectious, and I caught it. (Pip, on Estella: Chapter 8)

[It] was now too late and too far to go back, and I went on. (Chapter 19)

'You have been in every line I have ever read since I first came here, the rough common boy whose poor heart you wounded even then.' (Pip, to Estella: Chapter 44)

Summary

- Estella makes Pip aware of his upbringing's shortcomings.
- Pip's inheritance doesn't bring happiness, just unhappiness.
- Magwitch's return is a turning point.
- Pip feels guilty over his treatment of Joe, realising he has been arrogant.
- Pip learns that morality and kindness are more important than money.

Sample Analysis

Dickens presents Pip as having a **romanticised** view of life, seeing himself as a 'young Knight of romance' and Estella as the 'Princess'. This makes him seem naïve and innocent, but also portrays him as a dreamer. He has false expectations of his inheritance, derived from his own desires regarding Estella and his life as a gentleman. However, adult-Pip's narrative voice uses **irony**, recognising how innocent his younger self was and makes fun of him gently, in an endearing way.

Questions

QUICK TEST
1. What causes Pip's changed attitude to home?
2. Why isn't Pip happy after inheriting money?
3. How does Pip see Magwitch?
4. What does Pip learn by the end?

EXAM PRACTICE
Relating your ideas to at least one of the 'Key Quotations to Learn', write a paragraph explaining how Dickens presents Pip as a powerless character.

You must be able to: analyse the way that Dickens presents Magwitch.

How does Dickens present Magwitch?

Dickens uses **animalistic** imagery. Magwitch is like a 'hungry old dog' who 'snapped' at his food as though there is 'danger in every direction'.

Magwitch is 'in jail and out of jail, in jail and out of jail.' Dickens uses him to criticise the justice system that effectively perpetuates this cycle, trapping him. Having no home or education, Magwitch had no choice but to steal yet is harshly punished.

Magwitch's death is a criticism of the unforgiving justice system. Cheating the system by dying before it can kill him could be considered Magwitch's final protest.

How does Magwitch view society's hierarchy?

His determination to make Pip into a gentleman is revenge against the society that viewed him as worthless. Magwitch resents the prejudice that money makes people superior, the same prejudice that Compeyson exploits to get more lenient punishment. His determination in Australia is prompted by both revenge and generosity; he is triumphant: 'I'll show a better gentleman than the whole kit on you put together!'

How does Magwitch change during the novel?

Herbert describes him as a 'desperate and fierce character.' He demonstrates aggression (drawing a knife on Herbert) and desperation (in his 'ravenous' eating). However, Pip describes him at the end as 'softer', as though the satisfaction of seeing Pip has completed him.

Pip's understanding of Magwitch changes. Initially he sees a 'fearful man' who 'glared and growled' but when Magwitch is captured he describes a 'hunted, wounded, shackled creature', who is pitiful and vulnerable. Pip loves and respects Magwitch, who sees himself as Pip's 'second father'.

How does Magwitch change Pip?

Pip becomes more generous and kind. Deciding to help him escape demonstrates this change. Magwitch recognises it too: 'you've been more comfortable alonger me, since I was under a dark cloud, than when the sun shone. That's best of all.'

Key Quotations to Learn

He hugged his shuddering body in both his arms, – clasping himself, as if to hold himself together. (About Magwitch: Chapter 1)

'No man has done nigh as well as me. I'm famous for it.' (Magwitch: Chapter 39)

He looked terribly like a hungry old dog. (About Magwitch: Chapter 39)

I only saw a man who had meant to be my benefactor, and who had felt affectionately, gratefully, and generously, towards me with great constancy through a series of years. (About Magwitch: Chapter 54)

Summary

- Magwitch is described using images that show him as potentially fearsome, but which also reveal his vulnerable side.
- Dickens uses Magwitch to criticise the justice system that has let him down.
- Magwitch resents Compeyson, as he manipulated the belief that gentlemen are morally superior.
- He gives his fortune to Pip to revenge himself against the society which dismissed him.
- Pip comes to love Magwitch and see his humanity.

Sample Analysis

In the first description of Magwitch, Dickens' dual narrative uses the first phrase – 'fearful man' – to present the young Pip's fear, as Magwitch terrifyingly hides on the marsh and appears from nowhere. The contrasting following sentence – 'with no hat, and with broken shoes, and with an old rag tied round his head' – is a pathetic image demonstrating adult-Pip's understanding. The adjective 'broken' may apply to Magwitch as well as his shoes, and in the cold marshes, 'no hat' just 'an old rag' makes him sound dangerously exposed.

Questions

QUICK TEST
1. What imagery is associated with Magwitch?
2. How does Dickens use Magwitch to make a social point?
3. How does Magwitch undermine society's hierarchy?
4. How does Magwitch change?

EXAM PRACTICE
Relating your ideas to at least one of the 'Key Quotations to Learn', write a paragraph explaining how Dickens presents Magwitch as a sympathetic character.

Miss Havisham

You must be able to: analyse the ways that Dickens presents Miss Havisham.

How does Dickens use the Gothic in Miss Havisham's characterisation?

Physically, she is characterised as a 'ghost,' 'corpse', 'skeleton' – macabre images connoting that she is destroyed by her experience. Her appearance echoes her internal decay: she is rotting inside with bitterness.

Dickens uses the Gothic setting of Satis House to further show her decline. Everything 'had stopped, like the watch and the clock, a long time ago', including the rotten wedding feast infested with mice and 'speckle-legged spiders'. She is in Pip's nightmares; he **hallucinates** her hanging from a beam, and she speaks with 'ravenous intensity' that frightens him.

How is Miss Havisham manipulative?

She adopts Estella to 'wreak revenge on all the male sex', the society that failed her. Yet she is surprised and hurt when Estella is 'proud and hard', rejecting her too.

She manipulates Pip to 'Love her, love her, love her!' Hinting she is his benefactor further encourages him. It also torments her relatives to believe she's giving her inheritance to him rather than to them.

How does Miss Havisham function as a warning?

Miss Havisham has a twisted view of love, stopping time in Satis House and **saturating** herself in misery. She doesn't take responsibility, telling Pip 'you made your own snares' and blaming Compeyson and society for her situation. From her example, Pip learns to take responsibility for the impact of his actions on others.

How does Miss Havisham's character change?

Miss Havisham realises what she has done when Estella finally rejects her. She wanders in a 'ghostly manner, making a low cry', despairing over Estella's loss.

She asks Pip's forgiveness, giving him the money to fund Herbert's partnership in a gesture of repentance.

What is symbolic about her final moments?

She is set alight (it might be accidental or intentional; the ambiguity is deliberate). Pip describes her 'running at me, shrieking, with a whirl of fire blazing.' The fire causes Miss Havisham's death and destroys the wreckage of the bridal feast, indicating that the stopped time at Satis House will restart again.

Key Quotations to Learn

She had bridal flowers in her hair, but her hair was white. (About Miss Havisham: Chapter 8)

The bride within the bridal dress had withered like the dress, and like the flowers, and had no brightness left but the brightness of her sunken eyes. (About Miss Havisham: Chapter 8)

'So new to him ... so old to me; so strange to him, so familiar to me; so melancholy to both of us!' (Miss Havisham: Chapter 8)

The intensity of a mind mortally hurt and diseased. (About Miss Havisham: Chapter 38)

Summary

- Miss Havisham is associated with Gothic, ghostly or macabre imagery to highlight her moral, physical and intellectual decay.
- She manipulates those around her, especially Estella.
- She blames Compeyson and society for her woes.
- She asks for Pip's forgiveness.
- She dies as a result of a fire.

Sample Analysis

Dickens' Gothic imagery portrays Miss Havisham's decay. Her wedding dress was 'white' with 'bright flowers' but has become 'faded and yellow', **metaphorically** representing her decline physically, emotionally and **psychologically**. The change from 'white' to 'yellow' indicates lost purity, and her declining mental state. As a wealthy Victorian woman, marriage would have been her primary aim, and to be jilted is humiliating, provoking gossip that she was unsuitable for anyone else. Dickens' macabre imagery of 'skeleton' or 'ghost' suggests she is dead-in-life – the rejection has killed her.

Questions

QUICK TEST
1. What imagery is associated with Miss Havisham?
2. How does she manipulate Pip?
3. How does she represent love's power?
4. What is her turning point?
5. How does Dickens resolve her story?

EXAM PRACTICE
Relating your ideas to at least one of the 'Key Quotations to Learn', write a paragraph explaining the way that Dickens presents Miss Havisham as a tragic figure.

Estella

You must be able to: analyse the way Estella's character is developed through the novel.

How does Dickens present Estella?

Estella is characterised by cold imagery, having no heart, just 'ice in its place'. She is 'proud and refined' but also 'beautiful and self-possessed'. She is haughty, like 'a queen'.

She is disdainful to Pip because of his class and appearance, calling him 'boy' and insulting him as 'coarse' and 'common'.

Dickens associates Estella (meaning 'star') with the **motif** of light: she is Pip's guide.

How does Dickens present Estella's attitude to love?

Estella feels unable to love. She tells Pip she has no heart and 'no tenderness'. When she decides to marry Bentley Drummle, it is because she is 'tired of the life' she has led. Estella can't even love Miss Havisham, and explains the impossibility of this by likening her up-bringing to being raised in 'dark confinement' and then expecting her to enjoy daylight. She doesn't speak angrily but in a 'musing way, after another moment of calm wonder', as if it is interesting or unusual rather than upsetting; she does not seem to feel the damage done to her.

How does Estella change?

She becomes independent. As a child she follows Miss Havisham's instructions, trying to 'break [Pip's] heart!'. She later chooses to marry Bentley Drummle without consulting Miss Havisham.

She cares for Pip, as she knows she could marry him if she wanted but he is 'the man who would soonest feel … that I took nothing to him.' Bentley Drummle 'used her with great cruelty' before he died.

When Estella and Pip meet in the final scene she is 'saddened, softened'. She has a 'friendly touch' and has come to realise the value of what Pip had offered her, is able to recognise the importance of love, and is content to be friends.

Key Quotations to Learn

[Her] light came along the dark passage like a star. (About Estella: Chapter 8)

'Do you deceive and entrap him, Estella?'
'Yes, and many others – all of them but you.' (Pip and Estella: Chapter 38)

'I am what you have made me. Take all the praise, take all the blame; take all the success, take all the failure; in short, take me.' (Estella, to Miss Havisham: Chapter 38)

'I have been bent and broken, but – I hope – into a better shape.' (Estella: Chapter 59)

Summary

- Estella is associated with imagery of cold and stars.
- She is unable to love, raised to wreak revenge.
- She becomes independent, choosing to marry Bentley Drummle and rejecting Miss Havisham.
- In the final chapter she tells Pip they will 'continue friends apart'.

Sample Analysis

Dickens uses the motif of light to symbolise the importance of Estella, whose name means star, to Pip. When he is at Satis House he sees her come down 'the long dark passages like a star' then as he leaves she turns away 'as if she were going out into the sky.' These similes present her as a guiding star, and Pip follows her all his life as he wants to be worthy of her. The image of the star also implies her social superiority. However, she is a false star who will not guide him to where he should be. The light in the 'long dark passages' blinds him to everything else around him that could potentially make him happier.

Questions

QUICK TEST
1. What imagery is associated with Estella?
2. How does Estella change Pip initially?
3. How does she become independent?
4. What is her relationship with Pip like at the end?

EXAM PRACTICE
Using one of the 'Key Quotations to Learn', write a paragraph analysing the way that Estella is presented.

Characters — Joe Gargery

You must be able to: analyse the way that Dickens presents the character of Joe.

How does Dickens present Joe as a moral character?

Joe's good nature and kindness are crucial. Adult-Pip's narrative includes interjections praising him ('Dear, good fellow!') as he looks back fondly. He calls him a 'larger species of child', suggesting Joe's innocence.

Joe's goodness is seen several times. When Magwitch is captured, Joe insists he would have given the food gladly rather than see him starve. Joe's marriage to Mrs Joe also shows his morality. Mrs Joe is violent to him too, but he insists she is a 'fine figure of a woman' and a 'mastermind'. He is **wary** of treating women badly as he saw his mother 'drudging and slaving' for his father. His payment of Pip's debts and quick forgiveness of him in the final chapter is evidence of his generous nature.

How does Dickens use Joe to explore social class?

Joe has several interactions with the upper classes and is awkward every time. Dickens sometimes presents this humorously, when he plays with his hat 'like a bird's-nest with eggs in it, wouldn't hear of parting with that piece of property' or through his attempts to dress formally: 'he pulled up his shirt-collar so … that it made the hair on his head stand up like a tuft of feathers.'

However, Joe's clumsiness is embarrassing to Pip and makes the reader cringe on his behalf. He pronounces words incorrectly – 'architectooralooral', 'Miss A' – and retains his rural bluntness: 'I wouldn't keep a pig in it myself, – not in the case that I wished him to fatten wholesome'. Joe is very happy in his place in life. Ultimately, Pip accepts and loves Joe as he is, recognising his fundamental goodness.

Key Quotations to Learn

A sort of **Hercules** in strength, and also in weakness. (About Joe: Chapter 2)

'We don't know what you have done, but we wouldn't have you starved to death for it, poor miserable fellow-creature.' (Joe, to Magwitch: Chapter 5)

'Life is made of ever so many partings welded together, as I may say, and one man's a blacksmith, and one's a whitesmith.' (Joe, to Pip: Chapter 27)

Summary

- Joe is a moral character, acting as a father-figure who teaches Pip by example.
- Joe is working class. He is awkward and uncomfortable with the upper classes.
- Dickens uses language that reflects Joe's accent and dialect, to emphasise his rural background.
- He wants to treat women well, unlike his father's treatment of his mother.

Sample Analysis

Dickens presents Joe humorously, for example, Pip's description of him standing in front of Miss Havisham 'like some extraordinary bird; standing as he did speechless, with his tuft of feathers ruffled, and his mouth open as if he wanted a worm.' The simile makes him look ridiculous, his open mouth makes him appear foolish and stupid. The 'tuft of feathers' imagery makes Joe appear comical but also provokes sympathy for him because he is so uncomfortable in Miss Havisham's presence.

Questions

QUICK TEST
1. What are some examples of Joe's moral behaviour?
2. How does Joe's character reflect ideas about social class?
3. How does Dickens use language to show Joe's background?

EXAM PRACTICE
Relating your ideas to at least one of the 'Key Quotations to Learn', write a paragraph explaining the way that Dickens presents Joe as a true gentleman.

You must be able to: analyse the way that Dickens presents Jaggers and Wemmick.

How does Dickens present Jaggers?

Jaggers is often caricatured. With a 'bullying, interrogative manner' he 'throws his forefinger' as if interrogating people in court, 'he washed his clients off' and speaks in **hypotheticals** rather than giving factual information which could be **construed** as evidence. Dickens describes Jaggers as 'dark' and 'disagreeably sharp and suspicious', presenting his dubious morality through his appearance.

Jaggers wins every case but does not appear to care whether the defendants are innocent. He tells Pip to 'take nothing on looks, take everything on evidence', focusing on only what can be proven beyond doubt. For example, he shows off Molly's wrists as strong and vicious, suggesting he believes her guilt but defended her anyway.

Jaggers could be interpreted as morally corrupt. However, his character is **ambiguous**: due to his intervention, Miss Havisham adopts Estella, thereby saving Estella and preventing her from repeating Magwitch's life of poverty and crime.

How does Dickens present Wemmick?

Wemmick becomes one of Pip's closest friends. Wemmick advises Pip to find 'portable property', knowing that in legal cases such items are easily transferred.

He invites Pip to his home, a 'little wooden cottage' that he has constructed into a castle. This castle-like home protects him from his work, as Dickens explores the difficulties of blending public and private life. As he walks to his office he becomes 'dryer and harder' as he becomes his work-self.

How does Dickens present the relationship between the two?

They work together closely; Wemmick is exceptionally loyal. He understands Jaggers well, for example, when explaining his manner to Pip: 'he don't mean that you should know what to make of it.'

Wemmick keeps his private life separate until Pip reveals his 'Aged Parent' and Walworth home. This causes a softening in their relationship. Jaggers gently teases Wemmick about being a 'cunning imposter' with 'pleasant and playful ways'.

Key Quotations to Learn

Mr Jaggers's own high-backed chair was of deadly black horsehair, with rows of brass nails round it, like a coffin. (Chapter 20)

He took out his penknife and scraped the case out of his nails. (About Jaggers: Chapter 26)

[Whose] expression seemed to have been imperfectly chipped out with a dull-edged chisel. (About Wemmick: Chapter 21)

I saw Mr Jaggers relax into something like a smile, and Wemmick become bolder. (Chapter 52)

Summary

- Jaggers is connected to both Magwitch and Miss Havisham.
- Dickens uses Jaggers to **satirise** the legal system through his mannerisms and speech.
- Through Wemmick, Dickens explores the conflict between public and private life.
- Jaggers sees himself as rescuing Estella from a potential life of crime.

Sample Analysis

Jaggers and Wemmick both have ways of distancing themselves from the criminal world they associate with. Wemmick's house, Walworth, is a fantastical creation, which 'brushes the Newgate cobwebs away'; somewhere he can retreat to and be refreshed. It is the **embodiment** of the **idiom** 'a man's home is his castle' but surreal in a London suburb. The drawbridge 'crossed a chasm', symbolising the distance he keeps between home and work. Jaggers also has a mechanism for creating distance; he 'washed his clients off', as though he can remove his guilt with water.

Questions

QUICK TEST
1. Which of Jaggers' mannerisms caricature the legal system?
2. Why does Jaggers help Miss Havisham adopt Estella?
3. What is the conflict Wemmick experiences?
4. How does the relationship between Jaggers and Wemmick change?

EXAM PRACTICE
Relating your ideas to at least one of the 'Key Quotations to Learn', write a paragraph exploring the way that Dickens presents the characters of Jaggers and Wemmick.

You must be able to: analyse the way that Dickens contrasts the characters of Mrs Joe and Biddy.

How does Dickens present Mrs Joe?

Mrs Joe portrays herself as a **martyr**, seeking praise for bringing up Pip. She rules the forge through 'Rampages', angry outbursts, and violence, for example, when she 'knocked [Joe's] head against the wall'. Dickens presents her violence through ironic black comedy to diminish the horror of it – she uses a cane called 'Tickler' and Pip describes her playing the 'tambourine' on his head.

She is the **antithesis** of womanly ideals, unable to nurture Pip and Joe, and insistent on being praised for her dedication to them both. Pip describes her washing with a 'nutmeg-grater instead of soap', she is 'tall and bony' rather than feminine, and her apron is 'stuck full of pins and needles' keeping people at arm's length.

The attack on Mrs Joe leaves her dependent on others. She seems to be trying to name Orlick and shows every 'possible desire to conciliate him'. Orlick's attack is provoked by her lack of kindness, and her assertion of her authority over him in the forge. Her submission towards him afterwards feels more tragic because it's out of her character. When she dies, Pip realises she leaves a hole in his life as a mother figure, despite her harsh treatment of him.

How does Dickens present Biddy?

Biddy is a contrast, or **double**, to Mrs Joe. They are both domestic working-class women, but Biddy takes a nurturing role at the forge. She is Pip's confidante and conscience, asking him questions to provoke thought rather than ruling through aggression.

She meets Pip while teaching at the village school. Later she moves to the forge to care for Mrs Joe, where she **flourishes** due to the care from Joe she feels there.

Biddy is extremely capable; she learns everything Pip does by reading the books he reads, but remains humble and tells Pip 'I suppose I must catch it [education] like a cough'. Pip's surprise at her learning ability reflects Victorian gender stereotypes of women as less able, and in less need of education.

Key Quotations to Learn

Instead of lapsing into passion, she consciously and deliberately took extraordinary pains to force herself into it. (On Mrs Joe: Chapter 15)

The figure of my sister in her chair by the kitchen fire, haunted me night and day. (On Mrs Joe's death: Chapter 35)

She was pleasant and wholesome and sweet-tempered. (On Biddy: Chapter 17)

'Because, if it is to spite her … I should think – but you know best – that might be better and more independently done by caring nothing for her words.' (Biddy: Chapter 17)

Theoretically, she was already as good a blacksmith as I, or better. (On Biddy: Chapter 17)

Summary

- Mrs Joe is presented as the antithesis of femininity.
- She brings Pip up with violence and fear.
- Biddy is a double to Mrs Joe.
- Biddy flourishes at the forge, which is evidence of the impact of environment.

Sample Analysis

Dickens presents Mrs Joe's violent nature through the symbolism of her 'coarse apron … that was stuck full of pins and needles', which represents her lack of maternal feelings. Nobody can get physically close to her without being hurt; similarly nobody can get emotionally close to her. This contradicts the feminine stereotype of being nurturing and maternal whereas Mrs Joe rules through fear and aggression.

Questions

QUICK TEST
1. What are the similarities between Mrs Joe and Biddy?
2. What are some of the differences between them?
3. What is Mrs Joe's role in Pip's life?
4. What is Biddy's role in Pip's life?

EXAM PRACTICE
Relating your ideas to at least one of the 'Key Quotations to Learn', explore the way that Dickens presents Mrs Joe or Biddy.

Dolge Orlick and Herbert Pocket

You must be able to: analyse the significance of Dolge Orlick and Herbert Pocket.

What is Orlick like?

Orlick 'slouches', is 'dark' and speaks violently ('I'll be jiggered'). He is resentful and angry, believing he is treated unfairly. His physical appearance makes him recognisable later and reflects his inner evil.

How does Orlick's story interact with Pip's?

Orlick is what Pip could be if he had a different temperament. Although Orlick blames Pip and Mrs Joe for his troubles, claiming that 'you and her have pretty well hunted me out of this country', the truth is he has always felt entitled and resentful towards Pip. He uses the language of hunting, including calling Pip a 'wolf' and 'enemy' to dehumanise him.

When he attempts to kill Pip in a **melodramatic** scene on the marshes, Pip refers to him as a 'tiger', aggressive and vicious, ready to pounce.

What is Orlick's function in the novel?

Dickens explores fears that the working class are violent and dangerous. He is driven by revenge, attacking Mrs Joe then Pip. He refuses to accept responsibility for his actions.

Who is Herbert Pocket?

Herbert is 'frank and easy', 'cheery'. He teaches Pip manners, as though merely reminding him 'it is not the custom to put the knife in the mouth – for fear of accidents.' He teaches Pip comically, without judgement.

As Estella's cousin, he can tell Pip the truth about Miss Havisham.

What is Herbert's function in the novel?

Dickens uses Herbert to satirise the middle-class work ethic as he is 'looking about [him]' unable to find a profitable job. His character also gives Pip the opportunity to show his increasing maturity, secretly buying Herbert a job at Clarriker's. Once there, Herbert works hard and is very successful.

Herbert believes that 'When you have once made your capital, you have nothing to do but employ it,' to work on new ventures and explore new places, unlike Pip who sees wealth as static, to be closely guarded. Herbert represents the increasing capitalism of Victorian Britain. Having a job, demonstrating intellectual capacity and a strong work-ethic – the qualities and personality to enable one to earn – become more important than simply being born into money.

Key Quotations to Learn

He hammered it out as if it were I, I thought, and the sparks were my spirting blood. (On Orlick: Chapter 15)

'You was favoured, and he was bullied and beat. Now you pays for it. You done it; now you pays for it.' (Orlick: Chapter 53)

[A] natural incapacity to do anything secret and mean. There was something wonderfully hopeful about his general air. (On Herbert: Chapter 12)

Summary

- Orlick's physical appearance reveals his inner evil.
- Orlick represents middle-class fears that the working class are violent and dangerous.
- Orlick refuses to accept responsibility for himself.
- Herbert is cheerful and honest.
- Dickens uses Herbert to satirise the middle-class work ethic.

Sample Analysis

When Herbert leaves for the East, Pip feels as though 'my last anchor were loosening its hold, and I should soon be driving with the winds and waves.' The metaphor of the anchor suggests that Herbert is a positive force that keeps Pip safe. Pip feels he will lose his way and be buffeted by the storms of life as the **alliteration** of the 'winds and waves' makes them sound more threatening: he might be unable to keep his head above water without Herbert's help.

Questions

QUICK TEST
1. What is memorable about Orlick's looks and personality?
2. How does Orlick represent the working class?
3. What is Herbert like?
4. How does Herbert make Pip's life easier in London?

EXAM PRACTICE
Relating your ideas to at least one of the 'Key Quotations to Learn', write a paragraph explaining how Dickens presents either Orlick or Herbert.

Being a Gentleman

You must be able to: analyse the way that Dickens presents different interpretations of being a gentleman.

What is a gentleman?

In Victorian England, 'gentleman' indicated social class, mainly referring to a man who inherited class and wealth. There were also expectations that gentlemen would behave morally. Dickens presents different interpretations of 'gentleman' to question its true meaning.

Young Pip thinks a gentleman is someone with money, whose wealth is evident in their appearance. When Estella criticises his 'coarse' clothing and 'common' manners, he wants to be a gentleman to please her.

Who are gentlemen in the novel?

The 'Finches' are young and wealthy but often badly behaved. They are 'foolish', spend frivolously and argue. They are gentlemen in the traditional sense but not in the moral sense.

Joe is a true gentleman, being honourable and good-hearted. Examples of this are when he says he would have given Magwitch food, when he refuses money when Pip leaves, and quietly paying off Pip's debts.

How does Dickens use Compeyson to explore this theme?

Compeyson is a gentleman by birth who 'had learning' but becomes a criminal. He looks and acts the part of a gentleman – he is 'a smooth one to talk' and well dressed – but has 'no more heart than a iron file'. Dickens uses him to highlight the irony of trusting in appearances.

What is Magwitch's view?

Magwitch gives Pip money, buying the appearance of gentility, including extravagant jewellery ('A diamond all set round with rubies; that's a gentleman's, I hope!'). Pip's education is seen in his books ('You shall read 'em to me, dear boy! And if they're in foreign languages wot I don't understand, I shall be just as proud as if I did.').

Magwitch sees education and wealth making a gentleman, not heritage. However, Dickens presents Pip as a better moral character after he has decided to stop taking Magwitch's money, which suggests being a 'gentleman' is more about attitude than fortune.

Key Quotations to Learn

The plain honest working life to which I was born, had nothing in it to be ashamed of. (Chapter 17)

'You must be better educated, in accordance with your altered position.' (Jaggers: Chapter 18)

'No varnish can hide the grain of the wood; and that the more varnish you put on, the more the grain will express itself.' (Herbert: Chapter 22)

Summary

- Young Pip believes a gentleman is defined by wealth and appearance.
- He must learn that gentlemanly behaviour is more important.
- He has a good role model in Joe.
- Compeyson manipulates the appearance of 'gentleman' to mask his criminality.
- Magwitch gives Pip the money and education he believes make a gentleman.

Sample Analysis

Dickens explores the Victorian debate over whether being a gentleman is more related to attitude and behaviour than inherited money and status. When Pip joins the wealthy Finches, he describes a 'gay fiction among us that we were constantly enjoying ourselves, and a skeleton truth that we never did.' The **parallelism** of the phrases 'gay fiction' and 'skeleton truth' sets up a contrast for the reader: Pip knows that the expectation that wealth should bring happiness is false, whereas the contrasting imagery of the 'skeleton truth' suggests a dark hidden secret, reminding us that wealth does not make a gentleman happy if his attitude is poor.

Questions

QUICK TEST
1. What does young Pip consider a gentleman to be?
2. What lesson must he learn?
3. Why does he want to be a gentleman?
4. Who are some of the 'true' gentlemen?
5. Who could be considered 'false' gentlemen?

EXAM PRACTICE
Relating your ideas to at least one of the 'Key Quotations to Learn', write a paragraph explaining how Dickens presents ideas about being a gentleman.

You must be able to: analyse the way that Dickens presents crime.

How does young Pip see criminals?

Adults use the threat of crime and its violent associations to frighten him. Mrs Joe tells him the convicts in the Hulks 'always begin by asking questions', implying that Pip should remain silent or he too might become a criminal. Magwitch makes up a 'young man' who will 'tear him open', to frighten Pip into keeping him secret. When Pip meets Compeyson on the marsh, he assumes it is the young man – but adult-Pip's narrative suggests Magwitch is startled to learn someone else has escaped.

What social responsibilities does Dickens explore?

Dickens is critical of society for failing abandoned children such as Magwitch; without education or opportunity, Magwitch has no choice but to steal. Although he tries being 'a bit of a labourer, a bit of a wagoner' he can't make enough of a living this way.

Dickens also blames the justice system for failing Magwitch. At his trial he is judged unfairly, given a harsher sentence than Compeyson, who can look and speak the way a judge respects – suggesting that the law is more about privilege than justice.

Dickens is critical of the prison system because Magwitch is not **rehabilitated**. He has been read the Bible, but doesn't understand it. Because some Victorians believed in **physiognomy** – that a person's character could be ascertained from their appearance – he is measured physically. They also believed that nature, not nurture, was to blame for criminality.

How do Jaggers and Wemmick see crime and the law?

Both make money from the law's inequalities. Wemmick demands payment in 'portable property' before taking on cases. They use the injustice of the law to their advantage. Jaggers tells a witness, 'I want to know no more than I know', and witnesses are dressed more respectably and coached in their testimony. Wemmick contributes in part to the view of criminals as entertainment, by taking Pip to view Newgate Prison.

Jaggers' hand-washing represents his guilt in subverting the system and a metaphoric effort to cleanse himself from his work. Partly, though, he defends criminals because of the terrible conditions of the law and penal systems. He describes children 'held up to be seen', too small to see over the dock, and arranges Estella's adoption to save her from 'growing up to be hanged', a strong argument against the brutal Victorian punishments of hard labour, transportation for life and hanging.

Key Quotations to Learn

[As] if they were lower animals; their ironed legs … made them a most disagreeable and degraded spectacle. (Describing convicts: Chapter 28)

How strange it was that I should be encompassed by all this taint of prison and crime … like a stain that was faded but not gone. (Chapter 32)

'I was sent for life. It's death to come back.' (Magwitch: Chapter 39)

Summary

- Adults use the threat of crime to frighten Pip.
- Magwitch's story suggests that criminals are made, not born, not the other way around.
- Dickens criticises the lack of rehabilitation in the justice and prison systems.
- Jaggers' hand-washing symbolises his distaste for crime and his work.

Sample Analysis

Jaggers justifies the adoption of Estella by arguing he saved her from being 'imprisoned, whipped, transported, neglected, cast out' as child criminals were treated shamefully. It's a long, heart-breaking list that describes the lack of care, education and rehabilitation in society. The list becomes more fearful as it continues, from the violence of 'whipping' to the 'neglected, cast out' and excluded from all society, without hope of being able to re-enter it.

Questions

QUICK TEST
1. How does young Pip view crime?
2. What are Dickens' criticisms of the justice system?
3. How is Magwitch used to criticise the justice system?
4. What is physiognomy?
5. How does Jaggers see criminals and the law?

EXAM PRACTICE
Relating your ideas to at least one of the 'Key Quotations to Learn', write a paragraph explaining how the theme of crime is presented.

You must be able to: analyse which characters relate to ideas of revenge and what shape it takes.

How is Miss Havisham connected with revenge?

Miss Havisham raises Estella to 'wreak revenge' on men after being jilted leaves her with 'wild resentment, spurned affection, and wounded pride'. She raises Estella to be loved by others but makes her unable to return that love. Miss Havisham can't revenge herself on Compeyson so she targets all men, and the wider **patriarchal** society that insists marriage is the **pinnacle** of female accomplishment. She is humiliated and wishes others to feel as she does. However, Dickens uses her misery to show that revenge only hurts the person wielding it, as she has a 'diseased' mind and is without human companionship (including Estella, who rejects her).

How is Magwitch connected with revenge?

Magwitch takes revenge on society for turning its back on him. By earning his fortune he is proving that he is valuable to society, but was denied opportunity. He speaks with 'heat and triumph' about making Pip into a gentleman, seeing it as a personal victory for him: 'which on you owns a brought-up London gentleman?'

Magwitch also takes revenge on Compeyson, first by ensuring he is captured on the marshes: 'I don't expect it to do me any good ... I took him. He knows it. That's enough for me.' Towards the end, his fight with Compeyson leads to Compeyson's death – although this is not explicitly called murder (it takes place underwater so there is no evidence), there are strong implications that it was deliberate vengeance.

How is Orlick connected with revenge?

Orlick seeks revenge for his misfortune. He attacks Mrs Joe for treating him unkindly. He blames Pip for being fired from Satis House and being unable to win over Biddy, and attempts to kill Pip as a result. He also works with Compeyson to reveal Magwitch and ruin Pip. His determination ('I've had a firm mind and a firm will to have your life') has become an obsession.

Key Quotations to Learn

'That girl's hard and haughty and capricious to the last degree, and has been brought up by Miss Havisham to wreak revenge on all the male sex.' (Herbert, on Estella: Chapter 23)

'I bred her and educated her, to be loved. I developed her into what she is, that she might be loved. Love her!' (Miss Havisham: Chapter 30)

'It was a recompense to me, look'ee here, to know in secret that I was making a gentleman.' (Magwitch: Chapter 39)

Summary

- Miss Havisham seeks revenge against Compeyson, and patriarchal Victorian society.
- She raises Estella to be that revenge.
- Magwitch wants revenge for the way society privileges those who appear to be gentlemen.
- Orlick seeks revenge against Mrs Joe and Pip for mistreating him.

Sample Analysis

Dickens presents the damage done by revenge in Miss Havisham's claims regarding Estella: 'a warning to back and point my lessons, I stole her heart away and put ice in its place.' With the imagery of Estella's cold heart, Miss Havisham identifies the damage her desire for revenge has caused another human being, and the verb 'stole' implies that she knows she has done something wrong.

Questions

QUICK TEST
1. What is Miss Havisham's revenge?
2. What is Magwitch's revenge?
3. What is Orlick's revenge?
4. Who is hurt most in seeking revenge?

EXAM PRACTICE
Relating your ideas to at least one of the 'Key Quotations to Learn', write a paragraph explaining how Dickens presents the theme of revenge.

You must be able to: analyse the ways that Dickens presents different ideas about love.

What is Miss Havisham's view of love?

Miss Havisham has a twisted view of love as painful, 'self-humiliation' and deceit because of Compeyson's treatment.

She is tortured by Estella's lack of love for her. She realises too late that she has **estranged** Estella from herself because her love has been 'inseparable from jealousy'. In raising Estella in this way, she has damaged them both. She cannot find any joy in love.

What is Pip's view of love?

Pip's love for Estella is complex. As a child it makes him ashamed of his upbringing. His love for Estella could be seen as selfish. He believes Miss Havisham has intended them for one another, and does not consider Estella's feelings, only that she should fall in love with him to complete the fairy tale with himself as the 'Knight' rescuing the 'Princess'.

His love for her provokes 'agony' and 'despair', for example, when she marries Bentley Drummle.

However, Pip's love is sincere and he finds her in everything; 'on the marshes … in the light, in the darkness' and believes she's made him the man he is.

What is Estella's view of love?

Estella too experiences the difficult nature of love. She knows that other people love her, and she is aware she could marry Pip, but doesn't because he would 'soonest feel that I took nothing to him'. She is aware of the poverty of her feelings, using the metaphor of a child raised in 'dark confinement' and then asked to 'understand the daylight', and finding it impossible. She argues that she has been taught that love will destroy her and to avoid it at all cost, so Miss Havisham should not be angry that she can't love her. She marries Drummle although she doesn't love him.

Does Dickens portray positive impressions of love?

Joe loves Mrs Joe, looking up to her as a 'fine figure of a woman' and a 'mastermind'. He then comes to love Biddy, who tells Pip 'in a burst of happiness' that they are getting married.

Herbert and Clara also love one another happily and openly. They take Pip in towards the end of the novel when he finds himself penniless.

Key Quotations to Learn

'I have a heart to be stabbed in or shot in, I have no doubt ... I have no softness there, no – sympathy – sentiment – nonsense.' (Estella: Chapter 29)

'I'll tell you ... what real love is. It is blind devotion, unquestioning self-humiliation, utter submission, trust and belief against yourself and against the whole world, giving up your whole heart and soul.' (Miss Havisham: Chapter 30)

'Estella, to the last hour of my life, you cannot choose but remain part of my character, part of the little good in me, part of the evil.' (Pip: Chapter 43)

Summary

- Love is often presented as destructive or bringing unhappiness.
- Miss Havisham is destroyed by love and her response to this harms Estella.
- Young Pip's love for Estella makes him ashamed of his home.
- Adult Pip believes his love for Estella is an important part of who he is.

Sample Analysis

Dickens often describes love as difficult and heart-breaking. Pip says of Estella that 'I loved her against reason, against promise, against peace, against hope, against happiness, against all discouragement that could be.' The **anaphoric** 'against' makes his feelings sound like a battle to be fought. His list of comparisons – 'peace', 'hope', 'happiness' – position love as a contrast to these things, something difficult to bear. Although the final noun – 'discouragement' – is negative, he still wants to love her despite the difficulties that it creates for him.

Questions

QUICK TEST
1. What is Miss Havisham's view of love?
2. How does love affect Estella?
3. How does Pip respond to love?

EXAM PRACTICE
Relating your ideas to at least one of the 'Key Quotations to Learn', write a paragraph explaining how powerful love is in the novel.

Education

You must be able to: analyse the way that education is presented in the novel.

How is education related to social class?

Different classes are educated differently, which maintains social barriers. At the time *Great Expectations* is set, school was not compulsory in England. Pip is first educated at the village school, by Mr Wopsle's great-aunt who 'used to go to sleep' and by Biddy, who is only slightly older than the pupils. Pip does learn a little but finds it difficult as figures 'disguise themselves and baffle recognition.'

Contrastingly, some of the Finches are taught by Matthew Pocket, an Oxbridge scholar, with an aim to be able to converse on a wide range of cultural topics, but not necessarily learning practical skills.

Pip's education changes when he receives his inheritance. He is told, 'I should be well enough educated for my destiny if I could "hold my own"'. This suggests that being able to have a cultured conversation is more important than being qualified for work.

Characters like Magwitch represent educational failure. Biddy is also let down by the lack of systematic education in Victorian England. She is an 'extraordinary girl' who is 'equally accomplished' as Pip, learning everything he does ('I must catch it like a cough') but despite her brief role as a teacher of basic literacy and numeracy, she would never receive the education to do more.

How does Dickens use humour?

Dickens satirises the terrible state of education, like the village school's disorganisation and the lack of genuine learning that took place there. Pip's statement, 'We all read aloud what we could – or what we couldn't – in a frightful chorus', shows that understanding was not considered important. Biddy tries to keep order while the boys alternate between reciting from the Bible and stamping on each other's feet. This is **black humour**: although the image is entertaining, the lack of valuable education is partly why the boys stay in the same social class all their lives.

Key Quotations to Learn

'Why, here's three Js, and three Os, and three J-O, Joes in it, Pip!' (Joe: Chapter 7)

'I began to think her rather an extraordinary girl. For I called to mind now, that she was equally accomplished.' (About Biddy: Chapter 17)

'You shall read 'em to me, dear boy! And if they're in foreign languages wot I don't understand, I shall be just as proud as if I did.' (Magwitch: Chapter 49)

Summary

- Social classes are educated differently depending on their wealth and prospects.
- Pip is given a 'better' education, meaning more suited to his new class.
- The village school is humorously chaotic and useless, but Dickens is satirising the inadequacy of the education it provides.

Sample Analysis

Dickens is satirical when he describes the chaos of the village school and its lack of impact on Pip's learning: 'I struggled through the alphabet as if it had been a bramble-bush; getting considerably worried and scratched by every letter.' The simile of clawing through branches makes learning sound difficult and unpleasant. The verbs 'worried' and 'scratched' suggest that Pip must fight to learn everything, a metaphor for the challenging learning environment that surrounds him. This contrasts his experience with Matthew Pocket later in the novel who is 'serious, honest, and good in his tutor communication', helping Pip to learn better.

Questions

QUICK TEST
1. Why does Pip's education have to change after his expectations?
2. What does Matthew Pocket teach him?
3. What is Dickens saying about the failure of education?
4. Why does Dickens use humour to describe the village school?

EXAM PRACTICE
Relating your ideas to at least one of the 'Key Quotations to Learn', write a paragraph explaining how education is presented.

Forgiveness and Redemption

You must be able to: analyse the way that Dickens presents ideas about forgiveness and redemption.

What is a pilgrimage?

A pilgrimage is a religious journey, when a pilgrim travels to find inner peace and salvation.

How is this reflected in the structure of the novel?

Pip's journey is a secular life-journey. He learns the moral lessons of forgiveness, particularly towards Miss Havisham ('my life has been a blind and thankless one; and I want forgiveness and direction far too much, to be bitter with you.'). In turn, he makes mistakes that need others to forgive him.

Pip undergoes a moral regeneration, partly because of his acceptance of Magwitch. This is also symbolised in a Victorian **trope** of illness; when Pip is ill, he is suffering for the life he has led, which enables him to be cleansed and to move on. He recognises this is important in changing his views ('I feel thankful that I have been ill, Joe.').

Despite his earlier treatment of them, Joe and Biddy receive Pip with love, and he asks for their forgiveness: 'let me hear you say the words, that I may carry the sound of them away with me'.

Who else experiences forgiveness?

Dickens suggests that an essential part of being forgiven is asking for it, being able to repent and apologise.

Miss Havisham craves Pip's forgiveness, saying 'If you can ever write under my name, 'I forgive her,' though ever so long after my broken heart is dust pray do it!' He grants it almost immediately, realising that to refuse would be worse for him, making him bitter.

Magwitch's prison sentence should lead to social forgiveness but Dickens suggests criminals receive life-long punishment. Pip's affection represents Magwitch's forgiveness. He's happiest when Pip visits as Pip is 'more comfortable alonger me, since I was under a dark cloud, than when the sun shone. That's best of all.' He no longer feels he's being punished.

Key Quotations to Learn

'Until I saw in you a looking-glass that showed me what I once felt myself.' (Miss Havisham: Chapter 49)

'O Joe, you break my heart! Look angry at me, Joe. Strike me, Joe. Tell me of my ingratitude. Don't be so good to me!' (Pip: Chapter 57)

'Be as considerate and good to me as you were, and tell me we are friends.' (Estella: Chapter 59)

Summary

- Pip's journey is like a secular pilgrimage, in which he learns forgiveness and earns moral redemption.
- Pip mistreats Joe and Biddy but they forgive him by the end of the novel.
- Pip forgives Miss Havisham and Estella for their treatment of him.
- Magwitch is redeemed through his love for Pip and his dedication to him.

Sample Analysis

The changing descriptions of Magwitch suggest he has been forgiven. Pip remembers a 'hunted, wounded, shackled creature'. He was dehumanised and treated as an animal, 'hunted' and 'shackled' implying continuing imprisonment which, as well as the literal shackles, could be seen as the manacles of a **vindictive** society. However, Pip comes to see him 'affectionately, gratefully, and generously', adverbs suggesting moral redemption. Pip recognises the value Magwitch has added to his life. Although society has not forgiven his criminal past, Magwitch seems to have been redeemed and forgiven by a greater power.

Questions

QUICK TEST
1. What is a pilgrimage?
2. What is the significance of the novel's structure?
3. What is Pip's pilgrimage?
4. Who are some of the characters who are forgiven?

EXAM PRACTICE
Relating your ideas to at least one of the 'Key Quotations to Learn', write a paragraph explaining the way that Dickens presents different characters as being redeemed through forgiveness.

Parents and Children

You must be able to: analyse the different ways that Dickens presents parents and children.

Who are the absent parents?

Pip and Estella are both orphaned. Pip's impressions of his parents are sketchy, formed from the writing on their gravestones. He imagines his father as 'a square, stout, dark man, with curly black hair' and his mother 'freckled and sickly'. Mrs Joe has raised him, though not in a typically nurturing way.

Molly was accused of trying to 'destroy' Estella 'to revenge herself upon' Magwitch. The revelation is intended to be shocking, for a woman to become so twisted and obsessed by love that she would murder her own child. Yet Miss Havisham destroys Estella in a different way for a similar reason.

Who are the ineffectual parents?

The Pockets are comically useless – their children are 'tumbling up' accidentally rather than being brought up. Dickens uses dark humour to describe their ineptitude, for example, the baby is given a needle-case to play with to keep it quiet. Their wealth is protective as the children are safe and successful regardless. Matthew Pocket makes part of his living lecturing and writing 'treatises on the management of children'.

Who are the substitute parents?

Estella's adoption stems from different desires to save her – Jaggers' motive is to save her from a life of crime, and Miss Havisham wishes to save her from a fate like her own. However, Miss Havisham's misery leads her to mistreat Estella, bringing her up instead to wreak revenge on men.

Pip has several substitute parents. First, Mrs Joe, who brings him up 'by hand' and suffers the responsibility greatly. Joe is a moral father-figure, caring deeply for Pip and looking after him, conscious of Pip's good opinion. However, despite his love for Pip, Joe is unable to prevent Mrs Joe from mistreating him.

Magwitch, too, sees Pip as a son and works hard to provide for him.

Key Quotations to Learn

'I see so much in my poor mother, of a woman drudging and slaving and breaking her honest hart and never getting no peace in her mortal days.' (Joe: Chapter 7)

I saw that Mr and Mrs Pocket's children were not growing up or being brought up, but were tumbling up. (Chapter 22)

'I'm your second father. You're my son – more to me nor any son.' (Magwitch: Chapter 39)

'What were you brought up to be?'
'A warmint, dear boy.' (Pip and Magwitch: Chapter 40)

Summary

- Estella's adoption is intended to rescue her from a criminal life.
- The Pockets are ineffectual parents but the children are protected by their privileged lives.
- Substitute parents (Miss Havisham, Mrs Joe) can be unkind or cruel.
- Other substitutes (Joe, Magwitch) are more positive and genuinely love their adopted children.

Sample Analysis

Pumblechook tells Pip to be 'grateful, boy, to those that brought you up by hand.' His command reveals the Victorian attitude that children should be thankful to those who raised them. Mrs Joe brings him up 'by hand'. Literally, this means that she spoon-fed him after his mother died, and keeping him alive in an era of high infant mortality was something to be grateful for. However, Pip also sees the ironic pun as she brings him up with regular corporal punishment, such as the 'tickler'.

Questions

QUICK TEST
1. What are the reasons for Estella's adoption?
2. Who are ineffectual parents?
3. Who are damaging parents?
4. Who is the best parental figure?

EXAM PRACTICE
Relating your ideas to at least one of the 'Key Quotations to Learn', write a paragraph explaining the way that Dickens explores the roles of parents.

Social Class

You must be able to: analyse the way that Dickens presents social class.

What is Dickens exploring?

In the 1800s **contemporaries** like Karl Marx thought the classes were becoming **polarised**. Dickens instead explores how changes occur in people's class.

How are the upper and middle classes presented?

Miss Havisham symbolises fading aristocracy. She is an 'immensely rich and grim lady', physically separated 'up town' from Pip's village. The ruin of Satis, with its 'rustily barred' windows and 'grass growing in every crevice' represents the natural destruction of the aristocracy.

The Finches are unpleasant, overspend and are idle. Drummle in particular is 'idle, proud' and 'reserved'.

Matthew and Herbert represent the middle-class's 'cheerful industry and readiness'. Matthew makes a living through lecturing and writing. Herbert dreams of being a capitalist ('then the time comes […] when you see your opening. And you go in, and you swoop upon it'). Neither is wealthy but they are likable and honourable.

How are the lower and working classes presented?

Joe is presented very kindly. He is hard working and generous. He enjoys his trade, as seen in his use of blacksmithing metaphors when he visits Pip in London. Dickens suggests he 'fits' his place in society: 'You won't find half so much fault in me if you think of me in my forge dress, with my hammer in my hand.'

Orlick is presented as dangerous – unwilling to work hard, entitled, violent, drunk and vindictive.

How is class performative?

Class is performed by behaving (looking and speaking) a particular way. Herbert teaches Pip manners, but Pip is mocked by Trabb's boy, which reminds him his new status is an act.

Compeyson also performs class. Although he *is* a gentleman, he emphasises his appearance, manners and speech in contrast to Magwitch, which results in Compeyson receiving a lesser sentence.

What is Dickens saying about social class?

Regardless of class, those who work hard (Joe, the Pockets, Pip eventually) are rewarded and happy in their place. Those who don't, or who hoard their money (Orlick, Miss Havisham), are miserable, even dangerous.

Pip learns to work hard and be generous – the best combination.

Key Quotations to Learn

She was not beautiful – she was common and could not be like Estella – but she was pleasant. (About Biddy: Chapter 17)

'It is the desire of the present possessor of that property, that he be immediately removed from his present sphere of life and from this place, and be brought up as a gentleman.' (Jaggers: Chapter 18)

'[In] London it is not the custom to put the knife in the mouth – for fear of accidents.' (Herbert: Chapter 22)

[She] had grown up highly ornamental, but perfectly helpless and useless. (About Mrs Pocket: Chapter 23)

Summary

- Dickens explores how people's class can change.
- Class is often **performative**.
- The upper class is presented as unpleasant or foolish.
- The middle class is presented as industrious.
- The working class is either industrious (Joe) or dangerous (Orlick).

Sample Analysis

Dickens demonstrates the performative nature of class when Pip tells Joe: 'I wish my boots weren't so thick nor my hands so coarse.' His comments are about appearance and social behaviour rather than money, motivation or relationships. The adjectives 'thick' and 'coarse' are unpleasant with connotations of clumsiness, portraying Pip himself as roughened through work, at least outwardly. When Jaggers brings news of his inheritance he tells Pip he 'should have some new clothes to come in, and they should not be working-clothes'.

Questions

QUICK TEST
1. How does Dickens present the upper class?
2. What are the contrasting presentations of the working class?
3. How is class seen to be performative?
4. What is Dickens' overall message about class behaviour?

EXAM PRACTICE
Relating your ideas to at least one of the 'Key Quotations to Learn', analyse the way that Dickens presents ideas about social class.

Tips and Assessment Objectives

You must be able to: understand how to approach the exam question and meet the requirements of the mark scheme.

Quick tips

- You will be given one question on *Great Expectations*. There will be a short extract from the novel, followed by the question.

- The question will probably focus on a character or theme. Whatever its focus, you will be expected to show that you understand the novel's characters, themes and context.

- The question will have two bullet points. One of these will ask you to write about the extract and the other will ask you to write about the novel as a whole.

- Make sure you know what the question is asking you. Underline key words.

- You should spend about 45 minutes on your response. Allow yourself five minutes to plan your answer so there is some structure to your essay.

- All your paragraphs should contain a clear idea, a relevant reference to the novel (ideally a quotation) and analysis of how Dickens conveys this idea. Whenever possible, you should link your comments to the novel's context.

- It can sometimes help, after each paragraph, to quickly re-read the question to keep yourself focused on the exam task.

- Keep your writing concise. If you waste time 'waffling' you won't be able to include the full range of analysis and understanding that the mark scheme requires.

- It is a good idea to remember what the mark scheme is asking of you.

AO1: Understand and respond to the novel (12 marks)

This is all about coming up with a range of points that match the question, supporting your ideas with references from the novel and writing your essay in a mature, academic style.

Lower	Middle	Upper
The essay has some good ideas that are mostly relevant. Some quotations and references are used to support the ideas.	A clear essay that always focuses on the exam question. Quotations and references support ideas effectively. The response refers to different points in the novel.	A convincing, well-structured essay that answers the question fully. Quotations and references are well chosen and integrated into sentences. The response covers the whole novel (not everything, but ideas from different points of the story rather than just focusing on one or two sections).

AO2: Analyse effects of Dickens' language, form and structure (12 marks)

You need to comment on how Dickens uses specific words, language techniques, sentence structures or the narrative structure to get his ideas across to the reader. This could simply be something about a character or a larger idea he is exploring through the novel. To achieve this, you will need to have learned good quotations to analyse.

Lower	Middle	Upper
Identification of some different methods used by Dickens to convey meaning. Some subject terminology.	Explanation of Dickens' different methods. Clear understanding of the effects of these methods. Accurate use of subject terminology.	Analysis of the full range of Dickens' methods. Thorough exploration of the effects of these methods. Accurate range of subject terminology.

AO3: Understand the relationship between the novel and its contexts (6 marks)

For this part of the mark scheme, you need to show your understanding of how the characters and Dickens' ideas relate to when he was writing (1861).

Lower	Middle	Upper
Some awareness of how ideas in the novel link to its context.	References to relevant aspects of the novel's context show a clear understanding.	Exploration is linked to specific aspects of the novel's contexts to show a detailed understanding.

Practice Questions

1. Read the extract from Chapter 14 ('I remember that at a later period of my time' to 'I would feel more ashamed of home than ever, in my own ungracious breast.') and answer both parts of the question that follows.

   In this extract, Pip has just started his apprenticeship with Joe at the forge.

   Starting with this extract, explore how Dickens presents Pip's relationship with Joe.

   Write about:

   • how he presents Pip's relationship with Joe in the extract

   • how he presents Pip's relationship with Joe in the novel as a whole.

2. Read the extract from Chapter 8 ('In an arm-chair, with an elbow resting' to 'I should have cried out, if I could.') and answer both parts of the question that follows.

   In this extract, Pip has come to Satis House and sees Miss Havisham for the first time.

   Starting with this extract, explore how Dickens presents Miss Havisham as a tragic figure.

   Write about:

   • how he presents Miss Havisham in the extract

   • how he presents Miss Havisham in the novel as a whole.

3. Read the extract from Chapter 20 ('Mr Jaggers's room was lighted by a skylight only' to 'two casts on the shelf above Mr Jaggers's chair, and got up and went out.') and answer both parts of the question that follows.

   In this extract, Pip sees Mr Jaggers' office for the first time.

   Starting with this extract, explore how Dickens presents Jaggers as an intimidating character.

   Write about:

   • how he presents Jaggers in the extract

   • how he presents Jaggers in the novel as a whole.

4. Read the extract from Chapter 44 ('You will get me out of your thoughts in a week' to 'ghastly stare of pity and remorse.') and answer both parts of the question that follows.

   In this extract, Pip has discovered Estella is marrying Bentley Drummle.

   Starting with this extract, explore how Dickens presents the relationship between Pip and Estella.

   Write about:

   • how he presents the relationship between Pip and Estella in the extract

   • how he presents the relationship between Pip and Estella in the novel as a whole.

5. Read the extract from Chapter 11 ('I crossed the staircase landing' to 'she looked like the Witch of the place.') and answer both parts of the question that follows.

In this extract, Pip is at Satis House with Miss Havisham.

Starting with this extract, explore how Dickens uses settings to create a sense of atmosphere.

Write about:

- how he uses the setting in this extract
- how he uses settings in the novel as a whole.

6. Read the extract from Chapter 49 ('Yes, Pip, dear boy, I've made a gentleman on you!' to 'I shall be just as proud as if I did.') and answer both parts of the question that follows.

In this extract, Magwitch has just returned and revealed that he is Pip's benefactor.

Starting with this extract, explore how Dickens presents attitudes towards being a gentleman.

Write about:

- how he presents attitudes towards being a gentleman in the extract
- how he presents attitudes towards being a gentleman in the novel as a whole.

7. Read the extract from Chapter 27 ('Pip, dear old chap, life is made of ever so many partings welded together' to 'looked for him in the neighbouring streets; but he was gone.') and answer both parts of the question that follows.

In this extract, Joe has been visiting Pip in London.

Starting with this extract, explore how Dickens presents ideas about social class.

Write about:

- how he presents ideas about social class in the extract
- how he presents ideas about social class in the novel as a whole.

8. Read the extract from Chapter 42 ('I've been done everything to, pretty well – except hanged.' to 'I wore out my good share of key-metal still.') and answer both parts of the question that follows.

In this extract, Magwitch is telling Pip his history.

Starting with this extract, explore how Dickens presents crime as being a result of social injustice.

Write about:

- how he presents crime in the extract
- how he presents crime in the novel as a whole.

9. Read the following extract from Chapter 3 and answer the question that follows.

   In this extract, Pip has brought Magwitch some food on the marshes.

'I'll eat my breakfast afore they're the death of me,' said he. 'I'd do that, if I was going to be strung up to that there gallows as there is over there, directly afterwards. I'll beat the shivers so far, I'll bet you.'

He was gobbling mincemeat, meatbone, bread, cheese, and pork pie, all at once: staring distrustfully while he did so at the mist all round us, and often stopping – even stopping his jaws – to listen. Some real or fancied sound, some clink upon the river or breathing of beast upon the marsh, now gave him a start, and he said, suddenly, –

'You're not a deceiving imp? You brought no one with you?'

'No, sir! No!'

'Nor giv' no one the office to follow you?'

'No!'

'Well,' said he, 'I believe you. You'd be but a fierce young hound indeed, if at your time of life you could help to hunt a wretched warmint hunted as near death and dunghill as this poor wretched warmint is!'

Something clicked in his throat as if he had works in him like a clock, and was going to strike. And he smeared his ragged rough sleeve over his eyes.

Pitying his desolation, and watching him as he gradually settled down upon the pie, I made bold to say, 'I am glad you enjoy it.'

'Did you speak?'

'I said I was glad you enjoyed it.'

'Thankee, my boy. I do.'

I had often watched a large dog of ours eating his food; and I now noticed a decided similarity between the dog's way of eating, and the man's. The man took strong sharp sudden bites, just like the dog. He swallowed, or rather snapped up, every mouthful, too soon and too fast; and he looked sideways here and there while he ate, as if he thought there was danger in every direction of somebody's coming to take the pie away. He was altogether too unsettled in his mind over it, to appreciate it comfortably I thought, or to have anybody to dine with him, without making a chop with his jaws at the visitor. In all of which particulars he was very like the dog.

Starting with this extract, explore how Dickens presents Magwitch as a sympathetic character. Write about:

- how he presents Magwitch as a sympathetic character in the extract
- how he presents Magwitch as a sympathetic character in the novel as a whole.

[30 marks]

10. Read the following extract from Chapter 29 and answer the question that follows.

In this extract, Pip is a young adult in London, and is going to visit Satis House to see Estella for the first time since they were children.

> She had adopted Estella, she had as good as adopted me, and it could not fail to be her intention to bring us together. She reserved it for me to restore the desolate house, admit the sunshine into the dark rooms, set the clocks a-going and the cold hearths a-blazing, tear down the cobwebs, destroy the vermin, – in short, do all the shining deeds of the young Knight of romance, and marry the Princess. I had stopped to look at the house as I passed; and its seared red brick walls, blocked windows, and strong green ivy clasping even the stacks of chimneys with its twigs and tendons, as if with sinewy old arms, had made up a rich attractive mystery, of which I was the hero. Estella was the inspiration of it, and the heart of it, of course. But, though she had taken such strong possession of me, though my fancy and my hope were so set upon her, though her influence on my boyish life and character had been all-powerful, I did not, even that romantic morning, invest her with any attributes save those she possessed. I mention this in this place, of a fixed purpose, because it is the clue by which I am to be followed into my poor labyrinth. According to my experience, the conventional notion of a lover cannot be always true. The unqualified truth is, that when I loved Estella with the love of a man, I loved her simply because I found her irresistible. Once for all; I knew to my sorrow, often and often, if not always, that I loved her against reason, against promise, against peace, against hope, against happiness, against all discouragement that could be. Once for all; I loved her none the less because I knew it, and it had no more influence in restraining me than if I had devoutly believed her to be human perfection.

Starting with this extract, explore how Dickens presents attitudes towards love.

Write about:
- how he presents attitudes towards love in the extract
- how he presents attitudes towards love in the novel as a whole. [30 marks]

Planning a Character Question Response

You must be able to: understand what an exam question is asking you and prepare your response.

How might an exam question on character be phrased?

Questions 1–4 and 9 are typical character questions. Some may focus on an individual character and some may focus on a relationship. Remember that themes and characters are not mutually exclusive – a character question requires some discussion of themes and a theme question will require discussion of character.

Look again at Question 9.

Starting with this extract, explore how Dickens presents Magwitch as a sympathetic character.

Write about:

- how he presents Magwitch as a sympathetic character in the extract
- how he presents Magwitch as a sympathetic character in the novel as a whole.

[30 marks]

How do I work out what to do?

The focus of this question is on Magwitch and how far he is sympathetic. The bullet points remind you that you should divide your answer between the extract and the rest of the novel.

For AO1, you need to show a critical response, which means exploring what Magwitch is like, and to what extent he is sympathetic in the extract and the whole novel.

For AO2, you need to analyse the ways Dickens uses language, structure and form to show what Magwitch is like and to create sympathy for him. You should include some short quotations from the extract, as well as analysing Dickens' techniques in the rest of the novel.

For AO3, you need to link your comments to the novel's historical, social and literary contexts.

How can I plan my essay?

You have approximately 45 minutes to write your essay. You should spend the first few minutes reading the extracts and underlining or highlighting words or phrases that you want to analyse.

Then, spend a few minutes (no more than five) creating a quick plan.

You can plan in whatever way you find most useful: a list, spider diagram or flow chart. Once you have your ideas, take a moment to check which order you want to write them in.

Look at the planning example opposite.

Extract:

- animalistic imagery while eating
- clicking noise → dual narrative revealing crying
- looking around → unable to settle, feeling hunted
- dialogue – surprisingly kind to Pip?

Whole novel:

- childhood/upbringing – suggests an inescapable cycle of poverty
- repeats extract's imagery (dog) when Magwitch reveals himself to Pip; reintroducing the character and symbolising how little reality has changed for him
- ambition to create a gentleman – revenge on society that abandoned him
- makes fortune in New South Wales; determined and capable but lacked opportunity in England
- regular violence (Compeyson, language, lack of repentance)

Summary

- Make sure you know what the focus of the essay is.
- Remember to analyse how ideas are conveyed by Dickens.
- Try to relate your ideas to the novel's social and historical context.

Questions

QUICK TEST

1. What key skills do you need to show in your answer?
2. What are the benefits of quickly planning your essay?
3. Why is it better to have learned quotations, and aspects of form and structure, for the exam?

EXAM PRACTICE

Plan a response to Question 2 on page 58.

Starting with this extract, explore how Dickens presents Miss Havisham as a tragic figure. Write about:

- how he presents Miss Havisham in the extract
- how he presents Miss Havisham in the novel as a whole.

[30 marks]

Starting with this extract, explore how Dickens presents Magwitch as a sympathetic character.

Write about:

- how he presents Magwitch as a sympathetic character in the extract
- how he presents Magwitch as a sympathetic character in the novel as a whole.

[30 marks]

Dickens makes Magwitch sympathetic in the way he describes him, in the extract and the rest of the novel. He does this to criticise the justice system at the time. (1)

He describes Magwitch as an animal. 'The man took strong sharp sudden bites, just like the dog.' This simile (2) tells us that he is starving, creating sympathy because he has been mistreated in the Hulks before he escaped. This simile of a dog is used later to remind the reader that it is the same convict and to create sympathy. (3) Pip imagines him being violent and making a 'chop with his jaws', like a dog. (4) This links to him being violent at other times. He fights Compeyson on the marshes and the river. (5) Many Victorians would say this is because criminals like Magwitch are born evil, but Dickens uses Magwitch to suggest that people are made criminal by their upbringing. (6)

Sometimes the child Pip doesn't see everything but the adult Pip telling the story tells the reader. (7) When Pip describes Magwitch's sound it is like a clock. 'As though he had works in him like a clock, and was going to strike.' This means he is trying not to cry which makes him sympathetic because he is upset but trying not to show it because at the time men weren't supposed to cry. (8)

Dickens shows that Magwitch feels he is being hunted. He is described as 'staring distrustfully' and stopping to listen. This shows he's feeling uncomfortable and frightened, because he is also starving but he stops eating to check if someone is following him. He also calls himself 'hunted as near death' (9), which is a metaphor describing how he feels about the way he is treated by the prison system. There is more criticism of the prison system later in the book (10) when Magwitch explains his childhood. He says he has 'growed up took up' because he was arrested so much but didn't have any education or opportunity to stop him being a criminal.

Magwitch makes a fortune in Australia because he works hard, and he is proud of himself. (11) 'No man has done nigh as well as me. I'm famous for it.' He partly does this to revenge himself on society because it treated him badly and he wants to prove that he can do well, and that being a gentleman is not about being born with money. (12) But he also does it to reward Pip for his kindness. Dickens is showing that in Australia Magwitch has an opportunity to be better, but he didn't have this in England. Victorians didn't have many ways of changing the social class they were born into.

Another way Dickens makes Magwitch sympathetic is that he gives a fortune to Pip instead of keeping it. Magwitch calls himself a 'second father', the noun 'father' (13) suggests that he loves Pip and has tried to care for him like a son. Magwitch seems happy when he is with Pip and when Pip visits him even when he is in prison, because Pip is being a good son to him and showing love back.

On the other hand, Magwitch isn't always sympathetic because he can be quite violent (14), for example, when he raises a knife to Herbert or kills Compeyson in the river. His violence can be frightening for a reader.

Dickens makes Magwitch sympathetic to show that this should be different, and people should be able to change their lives. (15)

1. Clear introduction, which answers the question. AO1

2. Quotation and subject terminology, although the quote could be embedded. AO2

3. Some comment on effect. Could explain more how sympathy is created. AO2

4. Better embedded quotation. Could comment more on meaning. AO2

5. Shows implicit knowledge of the whole text. AO1

6. Clear relevant link to social context. AO3

7. Interpretive comment on technique. Could use subject terminology. AO2

8. Very generalised context; better to link to specific Victorian attitudes of masculinity. AO3

9. Reference a linked quotation to develop interpretation of idea. AO2

10. Explanation of context across the novel. AO3

11. Organised ideas. AO1

12. Clear links to themes across the whole novel. AO1

13. Use of subject terminology but not the most judicious choice. Labelling word classes is only useful as part of the analysis of meaning. AO2

14. Use of a counter-argument to show thoughtful interpretation. AO1

15. Concluding sentence relates back to the question and makes a final judgement. AO1

Questions

EXAM PRACTICE

Choose a paragraph of this essay. Read it through a few times then try to rewrite and improve it. You might:

- improve the sophistication of the language, using more varied vocabulary, and clearer expression
- replace a reference with a quotation or use a better quotation
- ensure quotations are embedded in the sentence
- provide more detailed, or a wider range of, analysis
- use more subject terminology
- link context to the analysis more effectively.

Grade 7+ Annotated Response

Starting with this extract, explore how Dickens presents Magwitch as a sympathetic character. Write about:

- how he presents Magwitch as a sympathetic character in the extract
- how he presents Magwitch as a sympathetic character in the novel as a whole.

[30 marks]

Through Magwitch, Dickens explores the way that Victorians treated criminals, and the flaws in their justice system. (1) Despite some violent outbursts and frightening behaviour, Magwitch is a deeply sympathetic character who was unable to escape the cycle of poverty he was born into. In this extract, one of Magwitch's first encounters with Pip, his hunger and extreme cold make him sympathetic. (2)

Dickens frequently uses animalistic imagery (3) to suggest both Magwitch's underlying violence and to create sympathy for his desperate situation. When he eats he 'snapped' with 'strong sharp sudden bites, just like the dog.' (4) The verb 'snapping' demonstrates his violence and aggression, making him appear desperate. The alliteration also exaggerates the violent motion, implying he's near starvation and uncontrollable. Later, in London, Dickens uses the same dog simile to recall this moment. (5) In Magwitch's retelling of his childhood, it becomes clear he has always been used to getting food where he can, not relying on its regularity. In the extract Pip imagines him 'making a chop with his jaws at the visitor', a violent sudden movement foreshadowing Magwitch's violent outbursts, including his fights with Compeyson on the marshes and the river, where it is strongly implied he is responsible for Compeyson's death. (6) Magwitch demonstrates further potential for violence when drawing a knife on Herbert when he feels threatened, on arriving from Australia. Despite his tragic background and generosity to Pip, Magwitch is capable of great harm, but Dickens suggests this is a response to his upbringing rather than an innately evil characteristic, as some Victorians would have argued. (7)

Pip's dual narrative creates further sympathy. (8) On the marshes Magwitch 'shivered' and has 'the ague', just one of many hardships. The word 'shivered' makes him seem vulnerable despite child-Pip's fear of him. The reader feels, as Joe does later, that no man should be left to starve and freeze to death no matter his crimes. Here, Dickens suggests the treatment of criminals is inhumane; Magwitch would rather escape to these conditions than be in the Hulks, the giant floating prison where convicts were detained. Child-Pip doesn't always see the full extent of Magwitch's suffering but the dual narrative shows reality. (9) He hears a 'click' in Magwitch's throat 'as though he had works in him like a clock, and was going to strike', struggling not to cry at his situation and Pip's unexpected help. This simile becomes a motif; Magwitch won't cry but the struggle to hold back tears in a supposedly hardened transportee makes the character even more human. (10)

Dickens uses Magwitch's story to criticise the legal and prison system. Even as a child he was 'put out of this town, and put out of that town, and stuck in the stocks, and whipped and worried and drove'. This syndetic list makes the process sound like a virtually inescapable cycle of poverty. The verbs 'whipped and worried and drove' also make him sound like an animal being herded through the system, representing the dehumanised way that many Victorians viewed criminals. (11)

Elsewhere, Magwitch is capable and ambitious, rising to wealth in New South Wales with hard work and determination: 'No man has done nigh as well as me. I'm famous for it.' (12) Although some of this work is motivated by revenge on the society that mistreated him, Dickens argues that, perhaps ironically, Magwitch had the opportunities in Australia he lacked in England – a meritocratic, egalitarian hope for society and an implicit criticism of the rigid social hierarchies of the Victorian era.

Dickens makes Magwitch a sympathetic character to criticise the Victorian social systems which created an underclass and excessively punished them for turning to crime when there were few options available to them. (13)

1. Links character with themes and historical context. AO1/AO3
2. Confident response to the question linking the whole novel and extract. AO1
3. Subject terminology. AO2
4. Precise, judicious choice of quotation. AO2
5. Links to wider novel. AO1
6. Shows confident knowledge of the whole text. AO1
7. Mini-conclusion to a paragraph, including a link to applied social context. AO3
8. Clearly structured paragraphing and use of complex subject terminology. AO1
9. Continuing to explore complexities of narrative voice, in a developed and sophisticated way. AO1/AO2
10. Evaluative judgement on creation of meaning. AO2
11. Connecting analysis to social context. AO2/AO3
12. Relevant quotation to support the point. AO1
13. Confident conclusion, linked to the ideas of the introduction. AO1

> **Questions**
>
> EXAM PRACTICE
> Spend about 45 minutes writing an answer to Question 2 (page 58).
> Starting with this extract, explore how Dickens presents Miss Havisham as a tragic figure.
> Write about:
> * how he presents Miss Havisham in the extract
> * how he presents Miss Havisham in the novel as a whole.   [30 marks]
> Remember to use the plan you have already prepared.

Planning a Theme Question Response

You must be able to: understand what an exam question is asking you and prepare your response.

How might an exam question on theme be phrased?

Questions 5–8 and 10 are typical thematic questions. Some questions might ask you about character and themes – but remember that any question on theme might involve some discussion of individual characters.

Look again at Question 10.

Starting with this extract, explore how Dickens presents attitudes towards love.

Write about:

- how he presents attitudes towards love in the extract
- how he presents attitudes towards love in the novel as a whole.

[30 marks]

How do I work out what to do?

The focus of this question is on how love is being presented, which in this case means romantic love as the extract is focused on Pip's thoughts about Estella. The bullet points remind you that you should divide your answer between the extract and the rest of the novel.

For AO1, you need to show a critical response, which means exploring different presentations of love, and how it affects the characters and plot of the novel, in the extract and the whole novel.

For AO2, you need to analyse the ways Dickens uses language, structure and form to show the way that Pip's experience of love is presented and changes through the novel. You should include some short quotations from the extract, as well as analysing Dickens' techniques in the rest of the novel.

For AO3, you need to link your comments to the novel's historical, social and literary contexts.

How can I plan my essay?

You have approximately 45 minutes to write your essay. You should spend the first few minutes reading the extracts and underlining or highlighting words or phrases that you want to analyse.

Then, spend a few minutes (no more than five) creating a quick plan.

You can plan however you find most useful: a list, spider diagram or flow chart. Once you have your ideas, take a moment to check which order you want to write them in.

Look at the planning example opposite.

Extract:

- motif of light – sunshine, destroying vermin
- romanticised, idealised 'rescuer' – sarcastic yet sad tone
- repetition of 'against'
- hopelessness of love

Whole novel:

- Pip's love for Estella changes his attitude to the forge – for the worse
- makes him arrogant/ashamed, especially when expectations happen
- causes pain to him – Estella's heart is cold/untouchable
- pain when Magwitch's arrival means Miss Havisham isn't his benefactor
- ambiguity of ending

Summary

- Make sure you know what the focus of the essay is.
- Remember to analyse how ideas are conveyed by Dickens.
- Try to relate your ideas to the novel's social and historical context.

Questions

QUICK TEST
1. What key skills do you need to show in your answer?
2. What are the benefits of quickly planning your essay?
3. Why is it better to have learned quotations, and aspects of form and structure, for the exam?

EXAM PRACTICE
Plan a response to Question 7 (page 59).
Starting with this extract, explore how Dickens presents ideas about social class.
Write about:

- how he presents ideas about social class in the extract
- how he presents ideas about social class in the novel as a whole.   [30 marks]

Starting with this extract, explore how Dickens presents attitudes towards love.

Write about:

- how he presents attitudes towards love in the extract
- how he presents attitudes towards love in the novel as a whole.

[30 marks]

Dickens presents love as being painful and hopeless through Pip's relationship with Estella and Miss Havisham's miserable life. In this extract, Pip is romantic with his ideas about love, but he knows how difficult it is. (1)

Dickens describes Pip's love as painful in the extract. 'Against promise, against peace, against hope.' (2) This repetition (3) of 'against' shows that Pip's love is hopeless. Because the things he is fighting against are good, it also makes his love seem negative. Estella looks down on Pip for being 'coarse' and he has rough hands. This makes Pip ashamed of his background and reject Joe and Biddy to become a gentleman instead. This makes him seem arrogant, even though he is doing it for love and a reader doesn't like that about him. (4)

Pip's love makes him who he is, but Herbert calls it a burden to him because he carries it like a 'portmanteau'. (5) Pip tells Estella she is part of good and evil in him, which shows that he doesn't know how to feel about her influence on him and that she has caused some bad things to happen. This could be a link to the way Victorians were religious and all had ideas about what good and evil was. (6)

Miss Havisham also feels painful love. (7) Dickens shows this through the symbol of her wedding feast which is rotting and full of insects. She describes love as being unpleasant. 'Blind devotion, unquestioning self-humiliation'. This is a very negative image, (8) as self-humiliation suggests that she feels guilty about being in love and what happened to her. Dickens also uses Gothic imagery (9) like the wedding dress that has turned yellow showing that Miss Havisham is also decaying. Estella makes love seem like a burden because she doesn't feel that she can love anyone as a result of Miss Havisham's treatment of her. She says 'there is no sentiment' in her heart. She knows when she marries Bentley Drummle she will not be a 'blessing' to him. This is sad, because Pip's love could have made her life happier.

Dickens uses the metaphor of light to describe Estella because Pip sees her as bringing light to his life. She is a 'candle' and he can bring 'sunshine' (10) to the house by loving her. This is like when he thinks that Miss Havisham is destroyed by not seeing the sunshine. 'Shutting out the light of day.' (11) Dickens creates a fairy tale between Pip and Estella. In the extract Pip calls her a Princess and sees himself as a young 'Knight' which shows that he is very romantic and has ideals about their relationship.

There are some happy relationships in the novel which show that love isn't always negative. (12) Joe and Biddy marry at the end which is a reward for their moral characters and the way they have been good to everyone around them – they deserve to be happy. Herbert and Clara are also happy when they get married. However, these are relatively minor characters and because they are at the end of the novel they don't have as much of an effect on the way that the reader sees love by the end.

The ending is unclear because it could be a fairy tale happy ending. (13) Dickens changed the ending to make it happier and more romantic, because Estella and Pip walk into the sunset. On the other hand, it is getting darker and Dickens refers to a 'shadow' which could suggest that there isn't a way for them to be together after all.

In the novel and the extract, Dickens presents love as being painful and hopeless, and the ending shows this because they might not be together after all. (14)

1. Concluding sentence is focused on the theme, with a clear link to the extract. AO1
2. Relevant quotation, could be embedded. AO2
3. Use of literary vocabulary. AO2
4. Detailed interpretation of the idea, showing knowledge of the whole text. AO1
5. Wider novel reference, could explain. AO1
6. Some reference to context, though not the most relevant idea. AO3
7. Topic sentence linked to the question. AO1
8. Interpretation of quotation. AO2
9. More useful link to relevant context. AO3
10. Embedded quotation. AO2
11. Uses relevant quotation, could be embedded. Interpretation with link to wider novel. AO1
12. Counter-argument to show varied interpretation. Could be supported with close reference or quotation. AO1
13. Link to literary context. AO3
14. Conclusion is relevant and linked to the question. AO1

Questions

EXAM PRACTICE
Choose a paragraph of this essay. Read it through a few times then try to rewrite and improve it. You might:
- improve the sophistication of the language, for example, by using more varied vocabulary, and the clarity of expression
- replace a reference with a quotation or use a better quotation
- ensure quotations are embedded in the sentence
- provide more detailed, or a wider range of analysis
- use more subject terminology
- link context to the analysis more effectively.

Grade 7+ Annotated Response

Starting with this extract, explore how Dickens presents attitudes towards love.

Write about:

- how he presents attitudes towards love in the extract
- how he presents attitudes towards love in the novel as a whole.

[30 marks]

Dickens presents romantic love (1) as a complex, often damaging, emotion. For Pip, loving Estella is always painful and hopeless, particularly when he discovers the truth about his expectations' origins. Nonetheless, Dickens presents the relationship in romantic ways as Pip's feelings are central to his growing up. In the extract, (2) Pip recalls visiting Estella as an adult and remembers the hopeless intensity of love.

Dickens presents Pip's love for Estella as painful. In the extract, Pip says he loves her 'against promise, against peace, against hope, against happiness.' (3) The repetition of 'against' contrasted with positive abstract nouns shows his understanding that love is a significant cause of his unhappiness. Love makes him feel worse about himself as Estella criticises him as 'coarse' and 'common', (4) creating shame over his background. This in turn leads to his rejection of Joe when he receives his expectations. Dickens' dual narrative creates pathos for Pip's sense of despair (5) as the adult Pip understands the 'all-powerful' effect she has on his life. This description has connotations of god-like control, which combines with the description of Estella as 'human perfection' to elevate Estella far beyond Pip's reach. Adult-Pip also refers to her influence as creating a 'labyrinth', suggesting that loving Estella has created a difficult path for him to follow to reach the 'centre' of his life (with her).

Dickens presents a highly romanticised view of love here and in several conversations between Pip and Estella. Here, Pip describes a fantasy of rescuing Estella with typically romantic conventions. (6) He is the 'Knight', Estella the 'Princess' and he has to solve the 'mystery'. This language implies Pip only has to follow the typical path to win Estella's heart, but a reader already understands that Estella is not the typical Princess waiting for rescue. This therefore creates a sad irony that adult-Pip can see as he looks back almost pityingly at the young Pip's naive fantasies. Dickens later uses romantic imagery when Pip declares his love unequivocally to Estella: 'on the river, on the sails of the ships, on the marshes, in the clouds'. (7) This anaphoric description (8) encompasses all the environments Pip inhabits; he sees Estella as being present in everything he does and is. She is 'part of the little good in me, part of the evil,' – the balance of good and evil suggests the internal conflict Pip feels for his origins and the aspirations she inspired. While they can be good, they have also led him to poor behaviour – to have a positive response to love he needs to find a balance.

Dickens presents the damaging effects of hopeless love through Miss Havisham. Being jilted at the altar was humiliating for her, particularly considering her status as a wealthy Victorian woman for whom marriage would be considered her major accomplishment. (9) She has been destroyed by the betrayal at her wedding. Dickens presents this through the symbolic ruin of Satis House, using the Gothic imagery of her wedding dress, deteriorating from white to yellow with age, and the decaying wedding feast infested with 'black fungus' and 'speckle-legged spiders'. Miss Havisham describes love as 'blind devotion, unquestioning self-humiliation'. These adjectives suggest she completely gives herself over to love, which destroys her sense of self. 'Blind' suggests it's impossible to see reality, meaning it's damaging and dangerous. Seeing love as 'self-humiliation' is tragic, partly because love should be empowering rather than destructive, and because the 'self' prefix suggests Miss Havisham has internalised the blame for the failure of her engagement.(10)

Dickens' ending is ambiguous regarding the outcome of love. Estella and Pip leave Satis together holding hands as though walking into a fairy tale happy ending. However, the 'evening mists were rising' and there is 'no shadow of another parting from her.' This could imply that the way forward for them is unclear – love continues to be difficult and create more pain than joy. (11)

1. Defining key words can be useful for example, 'romantic' is the focus of the extract. AO1
2. Connects extract and the whole text. AO1
3. Selective quotation embedded. AO2
4. Development of theme across the whole novel. AO2
5. Exploration of narrative voice. AO2
6. Reference to literary influences. AO3
7. Selective quotations from whole novel. AO2
8. Use of literary vocabulary. AO2
9. Reference to social context. AO3
10. Detailed exploration of individual phrases with subject terminology. AO2
11. Summative concluding sentence, confidently linked to the ideas of the introduction. AO1

 Questions

EXAM PRACTICE
Spend about 45 minutes writing an answer to Question 7 (page 59).
Starting with this extract, explore how Dickens presents ideas about social class.
Write about:
*   how he presents ideas about social class in the extract
*   how he presents ideas about social class in the novel as a whole.   [30 marks]
Remember to use the plan you have already prepared.

Glossary

Alliteration – a series of words beginning with the same sound.

Ambiguous – open to more than one interpretation.

Anaphoric – repetition of a word at the beginning of successive clauses.

Animalistic – typical of animals.

Antithesis – the direct opposite.

Autobiographical – using elements or all of the writer's own life.

Bildungsroman – a story about the experience of growing up.

Black humour – comedy making light of serious or painful subjects.

Callous – having an insensitive or cruel disregard for others.

Caricature – a picture or impression of a person with exaggerated characteristics for comic or gruesome effect.

Characterise – to describe the distinctive nature or features of someone or something.

Cliffhanger – a dramatic ending to an episode or chapter.

Connotation – a meaning suggested by association (not explicit).

Construe – to interpret in a particular way.

Contemporaries – people living at the same time as the author.

Contrast – to make differences obvious.

Doubles – two characters, or aspects of a character, being reflections of one another.

Dual narrative – a story told from two different perspectives.

Embodiment – a tangible form of an idea, quality or feeling.

Empathy – the ability to understand and share the feelings of other people.

Estranged – no longer close to or affectionate to someone, alienated.

Foreshadow – to hint at future events in the novel.

Genre – a literary style, for example, Gothic, romance, crime.

Gothic – a literary genre blending romance and horror.

Hallucinate – to see or hear something that isn't real.

Hercules – a demi-god in Roman mythology who was exceptionally strong but weaker than the more important gods.

Humour – the quality of being comic or amusing.

Hypothetical – a suggestion made as a basis for reasoning, without assuming it is true.

Idiom – a common saying or expression.

Imagery – words used to create a picture in the imagination.

Imply – to suggest something that is not expressly stated.

Interjection – an interruption.

Irony – using words that mean the opposite of what is intended.

Macabre – disturbing because concerned with or causing a fear of death.

Martyr – a person who suffers greatly because of their beliefs.

Melodrama – a sensational dramatic piece with exaggerated characters and exciting events intended to appeal to the emotions.

Metaphor – a way of describing something by referring to something else.

Misanthropic – having or showing a dislike of other people; unsociable.

Motif – a repeated image or idea.

Narrative voice – the way a story is told, that is, which person (first, third) and tense (past, present) is used.

Nostalgia – a sentimental longing or wistful affection for a period in the past.

Obsequious – attentive to an excessive degree.

Parallelism – when parts of the sentence or phrase are grammatically similar, one after the other.

Pathetic fallacy – either a form of personification, giving nature human qualities, or the use of a description of surroundings to reflect the mood of a character.

Pathos – a quality or situation that evokes pity or sadness.

Patriarchal – a system of society or government controlled by men.

Performative – using performance of a social or cultural role to create something, for example, an identity.

Personification – giving human characteristics to something non-human.

Physiognomy – the study of people's anatomy, especially the face, to determine character and mental abilities.

Pinnacle – the highest or most successful point.

Polarised – sharply divided into two groups or sets of beliefs.

Protagonist – the main character.

Psychologically – in a way affecting the mind or emotional state of a person.

Reflective – characterised by deep thought; thoughtful.

Rehabilitate – to restore to health or normal life.

Reminiscent – reminding someone of something else.

Represent – to stand for something or portray someone or something in a particular way.

Resolution – an ending that feels successful because the characters and storyline feel complete in a satisfactory way.

Romanticised – described in an ideal way, making it sound more appealing than it really is.

Sarcastic – using irony to mock or convey contempt.

Satirise – to criticise through humour.

Saturate – to completely permeate or fill with a quality or idea.

Semantic field – a set of words grouped by meaning.

Serialised – published in separate sections over a period of time.

Simile – a figure of speech that compares one thing to another.

Social realism – the use of real-life experiences or ideas in art for a political purpose.

Symbolise – to use a symbol (e.g. colour or image) to represent a specific idea or meaning.

Syndetic – using conjunctions between clauses.

Tragic – characterised by extreme distress or sorrow.

Transportation – the practice of sending criminals overseas for life rather than imprisoning them.

Trope – a recurring theme or idea, often a convention of a writer's work or a genre.

Uncouth – ignorant, lacking good manners or refinement.

Vindictive – having a strong desire for revenge.

Wary – feeling or showing caution about possible dangers or problems.

Answers

also include the unhappiness Pip feels, the alliterative 'self-swindler' implying he is fooling himself in pretending to be something he isn't, and the miserable adjectives and verbs ('dissociate', 'wretched', 'disturbed') when considering his relationship with Estella.

Pages 4–5
Quick Test
1. Joe Gargery, the blacksmith, and Mrs Joe, his wife, who is Pip's sister. Pumblechook is Joe's uncle. Pip is orphaned, with no other living siblings.
2. Pip meets the convict Magwitch on the marshes and steals food and drink from the forge for him. When soldiers take Magwitch, Pip tries to let him know he had nothing to do with his recapture. Magwitch takes responsibility for the theft of the food.
3. It is frozen in time; Miss Havisham wears an old wedding dress, and everything remains exactly as it was years before.
4. Miss Havisham asks Pip to play with her ward Estella, a proud young girl who delights in tormenting him.
5. Magwitch, who persuades Pip to steal for him. He fights with another convict, Compeyson; they both have escaped from the Hulks. The third convict meets Pip in the local pub and secretly gives Pip two pounds.

Exam Practice
Answers might explore: Dickens' use of caricature to make his characters memorable (for example, Mrs Joe's violence); the way sympathy is created in the simile of Magwitch as a dog with the alliterative description; the intrigue of Miss Havisham's setting, with the symbolism of white (purity) decaying to yellow with age, also a metaphor for her moral decay.

Pages 6–7
Quick Test
1. Guilty, because he doesn't enjoy it as he once thought he would – he's ashamed of how Estella will see him.
2. That he always keeps the name 'Pip' and never ask who his benefactor is.
3. Joe's other apprentice, a violent and resentful man, who is fired after arguing with Mrs Joe.
4. She is attacked and left for dead.

Exam Practice
Answers might explore Pip's guilt and dissatisfaction, including the comical description of Joe, which suggests the extreme difference in class. Analysis might include the past tense and reflective tone of 'uneasy' and 'sound' suggesting that Pip's life becomes less comfortable and happy.

Pages 8–9
Quick Test
1. Jaggers, Wemmick, and Herbert Pocket. He also meets Drummle and Startop who are tutored with him by Matthew Pocket.
2. Different family relationships – the Pockets are lovingly chaotic and noisy, the Havishams are cold and distant.
3. Pip is ashamed when Joe visits him. He sees Joe as clumsy, out of place, and uncouth. Joe recognises and accepts the changes in Pip.
4. She is more beautiful than ever, but cold and haughty. She tells Pip she is unable to love but he doesn't believe her. She reminds him of someone he can't place.

Exam Practice
Answers might include the greater difference between him and Joe, with the different settings where Joe is comfortable compared with his discomfort in London. Answers might

Pages 10–11
Quick Test
1. Early on Pip is a negative influence financially, but then he secretly buys Herbert a partnership at Clarriker's.
2. Mrs Joe dies, having never recovered from her assault.
3. They are from Magwitch, the convict who was transported to Australia but became a successful sheep farmer.
4. By the end he is miserable to think he isn't intended for Estella and was wrong about his benefactor, and is ashamed of treating Joe and Biddy as though he were superior.

Exam Practice
Answers could include the theme of love and devotion, analysing the obsession Miss Havisham expresses for Estella in the verb 'devouring' and 'reared' with its connotations of feeding on something, consuming it entirely. Themes might also include the question of money and happiness (the metaphor of 'skeleton truth', something dark and buried that is being uncovered, the contrast of 'gay fiction' and 'skeleton truth' to emphasise the way that people lie to themselves).

Pages 12–13
Quick Test
1. Compeyson pretended to love Miss Havisham, working with her brother Arthur to defraud her. Compeyson was also the other criminal who escaped the Hulks with Magwitch.
2. They look similar; he recognises Estella's face and hands in Molly's.
3. She marries Bentley Drummle, knowing she will torment him. She reminds Pip she was not built to love and always told him she couldn't return his affection.
4. She asks Pip to forgive her for the way she treated him.
5. Coals set fire to her dress and she dies soon after. It's ambiguous whether this is deliberate or accidental. It could symbolise her penance or punishment.

Exam Practice
Answers might explore Magwitch's upbringing, unable to escape the poverty of his childhood (linking to Dickens' social purpose) and analyse the contrast of clothing and his appearance as the 'slouching' fugitive. Analysis could include: Pip's description of Miss Havisham as 'diseased' through her own refusal to engage with the world; the metaphor of light as a healing force and the contrast with the darkness of Miss Havisham's self-imprisonment.

Pages 14–15
Quick Test
1. Magwitch is seriously injured and arrested. Compeyson dies. Before Magwitch dies in prison Pip tells him that he has found his daughter and loves her. He believes Pip will remain a gentleman.
2. Joe nurses Pip back to health and pays off all his debts. Joe and Biddy marry and have a son they name Pip.
3. He tricks Pip into coming to the marshes and tries to kill him. He admits attacking Mrs Joe.
4. They meet in the ruins of Satis House and agree to be friends.

Exam Practice
Answers might explore the idea that different strands are pulled together, including Compeyson, Orlick, Mrs Joe's death, and the ongoing friendship between Pip and Estella. Analysis might include: the pathetic fallacy of the weather as a contrast to previous miserable descriptions of the marshes, suggesting Pip's happiness with his origins; the philosophical tone of Magwitch's line with the imagery of water and the tide symbolising the inescapable passage of time, as well as his acceptance of his fate.

Pages 16–17

Quick Test

1. Pip as a child at the forge, Pip as a young man in London with expectations, and Pip's maturity after Magwitch reveals the truth.
2. A story about growing up, usually told in the past tense from an adult perspective.
3. To maintain interest for the next serialised instalment.
4. It can create sympathy by explaining young Pip's ideas or connecting events throughout the novel, or it can be comedic.

Exam Practice

Answers might explore the ways that Dickens creates humour and pathos, through adult Pip commenting on the ways young Pip behaves, or the way Dickens creates sympathy through the honesty of Pip's comments about wanting to improve Joe. Answers might also include the direct addresses to the reader ('it is the same …') to deliberately guide their response. Analysis could incorporate structure/form.

Pages 18–19

Quick Test

1. It is written in 1861 and begins in the early 1800s when Pip is a child.
2. The marshes echo Pip's emotions towards his home. Early on they are frightening and foreboding. By the end they are joyfully bright.
3. Pip's difficult period; his struggle with himself is reflected in the juxtaposition of death and crime, and the physical dirt and unpleasantness around him.
4. The ruin of Miss Havisham – it has decayed just like her mind and morality.

Exam Practice

Answers might include the different stages of Pip's life-journey taking place in different settings, or the symbolism of individual settings. Analysis could consider the symbolic pathetic fallacy of the marshes as 'angry', 'red', 'black' contrasting with the final description, or the metaphor of Satis House being like a prison, or the description of London's 'mud, mud, mud' using pathetic fallacy and listing to create a sense of dirt and despair. Answers might include Dickens' attitude to industry versus the rural environment.

Pages 20–21

Quick Test

1. Aged 12 he was responsible for the family as his father was imprisoned. He bettered himself through education.
2. Both worked from a young age. Both went to London early, and found they learned about society and the world there.
3. When novelists write about real-life experiences of situations, often drawing attention to issues such as poverty or working-class life.
4. Ideas about the treatment of criminals and orphans, the problems in the education system, the impact of the Industrial Revolution on rural and industrial life.

Exam Practice

Answers might include reference to the themes, for example, children, orphans, or poverty. Analysis might include comments on the cycle of poverty that affects Magwitch and from which Jaggers saves Estella, or the humour used to explore the education system, or the bleak descriptions of Newgate prison or the Hulks.

Pages 22–23

Quick Test

1. Often Victorians saw orphans as immoral, even criminal. They viewed orphans as being in need of correction to prevent them from becoming criminals in the future, but this 'correction' was often harsh or cruel.
2. To raise awareness of the difficulties they faced and create more empathy for the ways they needed to be brought up. By contrasting Joe and Miss Havisham, for example, he demonstrates that raising a child with kindness produces a better adult.

3. Victorians often believed that criminals were born, not made, and could be identified by appearance. There were harsh punishments, including life-long imprisonment and transportation.
4. Dickens suggests orphans can become criminals if not looked after properly, for example, Magwitch was stuck in a cycle of poverty and crime until he is transported to Australia.

Exam Practice

Answers might explore Dickens' social conscience and the contrasting experiences of different orphans or criminals in the novel, including their sympathetic representation. Analysis might include: Magwitch's dialect and dialogue, which suggests a personal voice/experience, including the negatives that demonstrate the lack of understanding of those in power; Jaggers' descriptions of children as 'spawn' in the 'net' or 'pretty little child' contrasting the two paths orphans might take; Magwitch's direct address ('till you put the question') challenging the reader to question their own attitudes towards prior criminals.

Pages 24–25

Quick Test

1. Meeting Estella and being called 'common', drawing attention to his background.
2. He doesn't fit in, doesn't work at anything and treats people with arrogance.
3. As a child Pip pities Magwitch and helps him. At first as an adult he is resentful and frightened for the impact on his own situation but eventually comes to love Magwitch.
4. To be independent and responsible for himself, to treat people fairly and respectfully, and that moral behaviour is more important than wealth.

Exam Practice

Answers might include the transition of Pip's life and how his attitudes change as a result of others' influences, for example, Miss Havisham's asking for a boy to play, Magwitch's fortune, Estella's torment. Analysis might include: the sympathy provoked by the 'bundle of shivers' suggesting his vulnerability; the disease metaphor in Estella's 'contempt', which is contagious and infects Pip with shame for his upbringing; the intensifiers in 'too late and too far' implying he has no other choice, and the permeation of his love for Estella into every facet of his life.

Pages 26–27

Quick Test

1. Animalistic, for example, comparing him to a dog, and the dehumanising language of hunting and imprisonment.
2. He suggests the cycle of poverty and crime is inescapable because of Magwitch's treatment by the legal system. He is successful in Australia, suggesting more opportunity in England could have helped him.
3. By creating a gentleman through new money, rather than via inheritance.
4. At the start he is violent and aggressive, even when returning from Australia. At the end Magwitch is 'softer', relieved and happy that he has made a gentleman. He is proud of Pip.

Exam Practice

Answers might include the way that Dickens uses Magwitch to criticise social systems (education, justice) that force children into poverty and criminality. Analysis might explore: examples of the dual narrative voice used to contrast images that create both fear and sympathy ('shuddering body', 'hungry old dog'); the adverbs (affectionately, etc.) describing Magwitch's behaviour in a moral and gentlemanly way, contrasted with society's expectations of who/what a gentleman is.

Pages 28–29

Quick Test

1. Gothic, including skeletons, ghosts, the ruined wedding dress, faded colours and the rotting wedding feast.

Answers

2. By pretending she's his benefactor, knowing the conditions of his inheritance and encouraging him to love Estella.
3. She is destroyed by it, remaining frozen in time and causing harm to those around her because of her bitterness.
4. When Estella rejects her as a result of her cold upbringing.
5. She asks Pip for forgiveness. She is set alight (maybe on purpose) – the fire is a purifying symbol that kills her.

Exam Practice

Answers might explain the way that Miss Havisham's misery has ruined her own life and Estella's, and that towards the end she regrets her treatment of Pip, asking for forgiveness. Analysis might include the Gothic imagery of decay and ruin, the imagery of faded bridal wear and setting, the imagery of the 'sunken' eyes like a skeleton. Her list using intensifiers to suggest her misery, and the metaphor of the disease she suffers.

Pages 30–31
Quick Test
1. Cold (ice in place of her heart), and light, including candles and stars.
2. She makes him feel ashamed of himself.
3. She chooses her own husband and rejects Miss Havisham.
4. She is softer, recognising how much he loves her and offers him friendship.

Exam Practice

Answers might focus on Estella's dialogue with Pip recognising her own behaviour but not in control of it. Analysis might include: the motif of light associated with Estella, suggestive of a guiding force (but that this might be misleading); the parallelism of her accusation (Chapter 38) blaming Miss Havisham for creating her. There is also pathos at the end with the alliterative 'bent'/'broken'/'better'.

Pages 32–33
Quick Test
1. Saying he would have fed Magwitch, his treatment of Pip, including caring for him when he's sick and paying his debts.
2. He is comfortable in his own environment and awkward interacting with others of a different class.
3. He uses phonetic spelling and dialect words to show Joe's rural background and lack of education, emphasising the difference between him, Pip, and Miss Havisham.

Exam Practice

Answers might explore: Joe's moral actions, such as his treatment of Magwitch in contrast to others' behaviour; his unstinting love for Pip, including paying off his debts at great expense, and his removal of himself from Pip's life when he realises that Pip has difficulty reconciling his presence in London. Analysis might include: the Hercules metaphor, combining aspects of the gods and humanity in describing Joe; the kindness with which he speaks to Magwitch; his analogies using his own experience with the contrasting 'blacksmith', 'whitesmith' to describe the differences that have emerged between him and Pip.

Pages 34–35
Quick Test
1. Washing his hands as though washing off his clients; 'throwing his forefinger' as if interrogating people constantly; refusing to speak facts that might be used as evidence in court.

2. To rescue a child from the life of crime he sees every day.
3. Trying to separate home and work lives, becoming different people in each place.
4. After Pip reveals Wemmick's home life, they are softer, smile and tease one another a little.

Exam Practice

Answers might explore their thematic links (Jaggers to criminality, Wemmick to appearances or secrecy). Analysis might explore: the **semantic field** created by the simile of the 'coffin' and adverb 'deadly' describing Jaggers' chair and the discomfort as self-punishment; the contrast in characteristics after Walworth is revealed with 'relax', 'smile', and 'bolder' suggesting a new stage of friendship as well as professional relationship.

Pages 36–37
Quick Test
1. They are both working class, domestic women, looking after the forge. They both marry Joe, and care for Pip.
2. Mrs Joe is forthright and speaks her mind, sometimes behaving aggressively. Biddy is kind, calm and reflective.
3. She's his sister and raises him 'by hand' after their parents' deaths.
4. As a young woman she loves him and tries to guide his conscience through suggestion and questioning, for example, when he is critical of Joe. Later, she marries Joe.

Exam Practice

Answers might explore the contrasting impressions or their doubling. Analysis might include: the contrast between Mrs Joe's violent attitude towards Pip, in the adverbs 'consciously and deliberately' to describe her reaction, to create drama, with Pip's unexpected grief through the verb 'haunted' as though he cannot forget her; Biddy's tentative nature when giving (sensible) advice; the way Pip expresses admiration for Biddy's ability.

Pages 38–39
Quick Test
1. He is dark and slouching, an outward indication of his evil and resentful personality.
2. He is often drunk and resentful, feeling entitled to better things, rather than hard working. He believes the world treats him badly, and is violent and unpleasant as a result.
3. He is kind, generous, hard working. He 'looks about him' ineffectually but once at Clarriker's is a positive role model.
4. He teaches Pip manners, joining the Finches with him, giving him advice. He supports Pip in helping Magwitch to try to escape the country.

Exam Practice

Answers might explore Orlick's misanthropic characterisation, particularly the non-standard grammar to symbolise his working-class nature. Analysis might explore the violence of 'spirting blood' foreshadowing Orlick's murderous intentions, and his accusatory language towards Pip. Analysis of Herbert might include the adjectival phrases 'wonderfully hopeful' and 'natural incapacity' for meanness to describe his innate goodness.

Pages 40–41
Quick Test
1. As a young boy, Pip thinks being a gentleman relates to money and appearance, rather than behaviour.
2. That gentlemanly behaviour is more important.
3. To be worthy of Estella.
4. Joe Gargery and Herbert Pocket.
5. Compeyson and the Finches.

Exam Practice

Answers might explore the opposing views of what a gentleman is, and Pip's journey to understanding. Analysis might explore: the varnish metaphor, in relation to Compeyson; the adjectives 'better' and 'altered', implying that education is only suitable for some people or the positive language 'plain honest' in conjunction with rural life rather than high social class, reflecting the idea that the poorest people in the novel are often the happiest.

Pages 42–43
Quick Test
1. Adults use crime to terrify him into behaving well. He sees his taking the food for Magwitch as a crime worthy of the Hulks – there's no scale of severity.
2. It doesn't rehabilitate and can make the cycle worse by not treating criminals like human beings.
3. His life leads him into crime; the justice system treats him and Compeyson differently because of their outward appearances not their relative guilt; there are no real ways to rehabilitate or educate him in prison.
4. The practice of examining anatomy, particularly facial characteristics, to predict people's characters and morality.
5. He regularly washes his hands, showing distaste. But he also pities criminals, defending them regardless of guilt, partly for money but also because of their terrible treatment by the system.

Exam Practice
Answers might explore Dickens' social exploration of nature versus nurture, or the seemingly inescapable cycle of poverty and crime, and the treatment of criminals. Analysis could consider: the dehumanising of criminals by the use of animal imagery and the noun 'spectacle' to describe them as something bizarre to be watched; the language 'taint'/'faded' as though crime is always present and cannot be fully erased; the harsh punishments and Magwitch's blunt statement 'It's death to come back', which indicates lack of forgiveness in the system.

Pages 44–45
Quick Test
1. Raising Estella to be loved but unable to love (her revenge on Compeyson in particular and on men in general).
2. Creating a gentleman in Pip (his revenge on society).
3. Attacking Mrs Joe, revealing Magwitch and trying to kill Pip (his revenge on Mrs Joe, Magwitch and Pip).
4. The person seeking revenge (Magwitch is ambiguous; although he dies, he remains proud and loving towards Pip and happy with his accomplishment).

Exam Practice
Answers might explore different characters' motives and ways of seeking revenge, including Orlick, Magwitch, and Miss Havisham. Analysis might explore: the repetition and exclamation showing Miss Havisham's uncontrollable rage; the descriptions of Estella as cold and hard as a result of Miss Havisham's revenge; the comparison Magwitch makes between himself and others, calling it 'recompense' as though it is his right or repayment for his mistreatment.

Pages 46–47
Quick Test
1. That love destroys, and she ruins Estella as a result.
2. She is unable to love, even her adopted mother, and is cold towards everyone.
3. Unhappily. It causes him to be ashamed of his life, and even in London he is miserable because Estella's treatment of him does not match his hopes.

Exam Practice
Answers might explore the destructive force of love on Miss Havisham and Estella, as well as Pip in his misery. Analysis might include: the regular juxtaposition of love and hate; the listing of 'against' implying the futility of love; Miss Havisham's extremely negative language including the idea of 'self-humiliation' with the prefix blaming herself (not Compeyson) for what happened; Pip's balancing of good and evil in his experience of love; the definitive tone of Estella's 'nonsense' as she calls love.

Pages 48–49
Quick Test
1. Different classes have different educations, whether providing practical, basic literacy, or cultural knowledge. The village school isn't good enough for Pip's future social status.
2. Social and cultural knowledge, so he can participate in conversations with those of similar status.
3. That the poor are uneducated, which keeps them where they are and restricts their opportunities, but also that boys like the Finches don't need preparation for a working life (i.e. a trade or profession) because of their inherited wealth.
4. To make the reader think about the difference between what is being learned and what could be learned, and to see the chaos when education is provided this way.

Exam Practice
Answers might explore the different educations received in the novel, analysing Joe's happiness in his exclamation, and that his skill in the forge perhaps seems less valued (suggestive of Pip's changed attitude). Analysis might include: the dialect of Magwitch, and the pride expressed in his quotation, seeing a language as evidence of learning regardless of understanding; Biddy's comparative lack of opportunity and the positive adjectives 'accomplished' and 'extraordinary' to explain her ability to learn.

Pages 50–51
Quick Test
1. A religious journey ending in inner peace.
2. He undergoes a secular journey, learning moral redemption.
3. He undergoes moral regeneration and is received back into his family with love.
4. Miss Havisham, Pip, Magwitch, Estella.

Exam Practice
Answers might explore the ways characters have sinned and the ways in which they ask for forgiveness and receive it. Analysis might include: the 'looking glass' metaphor, implying that Miss Havisham sees herself clearly for the first time; Pip's exclamations suggesting he feels undeserving of forgiveness; Estella's imperative, not asking for love but friendship instead. Answers could begin to consider whether forgiveness is enough for redemption or whether, as in Miss Havisham's and Pip's case, an external force can demonstrate redemption (the fire, his illness).

Pages 52–53
Quick Test
1. Jaggers arranges it to prevent her from following the life of Molly and Magwitch. Miss Havisham wants a girl to bring up to save her from repeating her own fate.
2. The Pockets, not truly guiding their children. Joe is kind, but can't prevent Mrs Joe's cruelty towards Pip.
3. Miss Havisham damages Estella's ability to love, Mrs Joe is violent towards Pip, Molly and Magwitch are potentially poor parents because of their situation and criminal background.
4. Perhaps Magwitch, for providing financially (and as a role model, in later life) for Pip, or Joe, unwavering in love and support.

Exam Practice
Answers might explore the contrasting styles of parenting and how their children are brought up as a result, either hands-off (like the Pockets, useless but kind, Magwitch's cruel abandonment by his parents), or involved although cruel (Miss Havisham) or unkind (Mrs Joe). Parenthood might be explored as a set of moral responsibilities unrelated to biology, for example, Joe's unwavering love for Pip. Analysis might include: the comic verb phrase 'tumbling up', indicating a lack of guidance; the repetition of 'son' to emphasise Magwitch's love for Pip; Joe's syndetic list demonstrating the example he had, and the reason he feels compelled to care for Mrs Joe even though her treatment of Pip was unkind.

Answers

Pages 54–55

Quick Test

1. The upper class could be proud, selfish and uncaring or cruel (Miss Havisham, the Finches). The middle-class Pockets are kind and hard working although sometimes foolish.
2. Joe is presented positively – hard working, kind, generous and moral. Orlick is a negative representation, feeling resentful and entitled. He is dangerous and often drunk or violent.
3. Class is associated with appearance, for example, Compeyson's 'gentlemanly' speech, manners and clothing earn him a lesser sentence than Magwitch. Pip's first awareness of his lower-class status is through his appearance (hands) and speech (calling 'knaves' 'jacks').
4. Hard work and generosity are morally more important than (inherited) wealth, and those who work hard are rewarded accordingly. It is important to behave authentically, rather than perform as a class type.

Exam Practice

Answers might explore the contrasting views of class, and the complexities of class and hard work. Analysis might explore: the adverb 'immediately' suggesting urgency as though Pip can't fulfil his new role in his current location; the hedged advice Herbert gives, which is polite but demonstrates different social mannerisms; the contrast between the 'ornamental' Mrs Pocket, implying her beauty but lack of function, with Biddy as 'not beautiful', implying a working-class girl cannot be more than 'pleasant'.

Pages 62–63

Quick Test

1. Understanding of the whole text, specific analysis and terminology, awareness of the relevance of context, a well-structured essay and accurate writing.
2. Planning focuses your thoughts and allows you to produce a well-structured essay.

3. To enable you to do specific AO2 analysis.

Exam Practice

Ideas might include: Miss Havisham's treatment of Estella and Pip, because of her own misery and resentment; the way that Dickens describes her appearance with Gothic imagery, reference to death, decay and waxworks; the association of Miss Havisham with nightmares and hallucinations; her cruelty to Pip followed by her money for Herbert and desire for forgiveness.

Pages 68–69

Quick Test

1. Understanding of the whole text, specific analysis and terminology, awareness of the relevance of context, a well-structured essay and accurate writing.
2. Planning focuses your thoughts and allows you to produce a well-structured essay.
3. To enable you to do specific AO2 analysis.

Exam Practice

Ideas might include: the ways in which Dickens presents different classes, suggesting they cannot be comfortable in one another's situations, and how Dickens presents hard work and kindness as preferable to concerns about status, romanticising this in the working class. Analysis of the extract might include: Joe's use of 'smithing' language implying his expertise in his craft; the repetition of 'wrong' emphasising where he feels most comfortable (and linking to the wider novel where he feels awkward, for example, with Miss Havisham, addressing Pip instead of speaking to her, or playing with his hat in front of Herbert); Joe's moral goodness in saying goodbye to Pip without anger, and the physical representation of him in 'forge dress' with the 'hammer' or 'pipe' as the hallmarks of his class. Comments on the wider novel might contrast him with Orlick's dangerous nature, or with the unpleasantness of the upper class such as Bentley Drummle.

Pages 66–67 and pages 72–73

Use the mark scheme below to self-assess your strengths and weaknesses. Work up from the bottom, putting a tick by things you have fully accomplished, a ½ by skills that are in place but need securing and underlining areas that need development. The estimated grade boundaries are included so you can assess your progress towards your target grade.

Grade	AO1 (12 marks)	AO2 (12 marks)	AO3 (6 marks)
6–7+	A convincing, well-structured essay that answers the question fully. Quotations and references are well chosen and integrated into sentences. The response covers the whole novel.	Analysis of the full range of Dickens' methods. Thorough exploration of the effects of these methods. Accurate range of subject terminology.	Exploration is linked to specific aspects of the novel's contexts to show detailed understanding.
4–5	A clear essay that always focuses on the exam question. Quotations and references support ideas effectively. The response refers to different points in the novel.	Explanation of Dickens' different methods. Clear understanding of the effects of these methods. Accurate use of subject terminology.	References to relevant aspects of context show clear understanding.
2–3	The essay has some good ideas that are mostly relevant. Some quotations and references are used to support the ideas.	Identification of some different methods used by Dickens to convey meaning. Some subject terminology.	Some awareness of how ideas in the novel link to its context.